THE
AGED
IN
RURAL
AMERICA

Recent Titles in
Contributions to the Study of Aging

Geriatric Medicine in the United States and Great Britain
David K. Carboni

Innovative Aging Programs Abroad: Implications for the United
States
Charlotte Nusberg, with Mary Jo Gibson and Sheila Peace

The Extreme Aged in America: A Portrait of an Expanding
Population
Ira Rosenwaike, with the assistance of Barbara Logue

Old Age in a Bureaucratic Society: The Elderly, the Experts, and the
State in American History
David Van Tassel and Peter N. Stearns, editors

THE
AGED
IN
RURAL
AMERICA

JOHN A. KROUT

Contributions to the Study of Aging,
Number 5

GREENWOOD PRESS
New York • Westport, Connecticut • London

Library of Congress Cataloging-in-Publication Data

Krout, John A.
  The aged in rural America.

  (Contributions to the study of aging, ISSN 0732–085X; no. 5)
  Bibliography: p.
  Includes index.
  1. Rural aged—United States.   2. Aged—United States.
I. Title.   II. Series.
HQ1064.U5K75   1986   305.2′6′0973   85–17740
ISBN 0–313–24511–8 (lib. bdg. : alk. paper)

Library of Congress Catalog Card Number: 85–17740
ISBN: 0–313–24511–8
ISSN: 0732–085X

First published in 1986

Greenwood Press, Inc.
88 Post Road West
Westport, Connecticut 06881

Printed in the United States of America

The paper used in this book complies with the
Permanent Paper Standard issued by the National
Information Standards Organization (Z39.48–1984).

10 9 8 7 6 5 4 3 2 1

CONTENTS

Tables   xi

Preface   xiii

Acknowledgments   xv

1 Introduction   1

Goal of Book   1
Definition of "Rural"   2
Rural/Urban Differences   3
  Values   4
  Physical Differences   5
Some Guiding Observations   6
  Variability Among the Rural Elderly   6
  Disadvantaged Status of the Rural Elderly   7
  Rural Elderly Needs Assessment Literature   8
  Life Satisfaction of the Rural Elderly   8
Organization of Book   9
References   10

2 Demographic Characteristics   15

Introduction   15
How Many Rural Elderly?   16
Geographic Distribution   19

Socio-Demographic Characteristics   22
   Racial Differences   22
   Sex Differences   24
   Marital Status Differences   24
   Family Status Differences   26
Trends in Size of Rural Elderly Population   27
Nonmetropolitan Population Turnaround   27
Consequences of Rural Elderly Increase   31
Research Needs   32
Summary   33
References   35

3 Economic Status   39

Introduction   39
Rural Versus Urban Elderly Income Differences   40
Poverty Among the Rural Elderly   41
Income As an Indicator of Economic Well-Being   43
Perception of Income Adequacy   45
Research Needs   47
Summary   48
References   49

4 Work, Retirement, and Leisure   51

Introduction   51
Employment Status   52
Work Satisfaction   53
Retirement   54
Retirement Satisfaction   55
Leisure   56
Leisure/Recreation Services   59
Research Needs   61
Summary   62
References   63

5 Physical Health   67

Introduction   67
Health Status   68
Rural/Urban Elderly Health Differences   70
Nutritional Status   73
Self-Assessed Health   74

Health Care   75
Obstacles to Health Care   78
Research Needs   79
Summary   81
References   82

6 Mental Health   87

Introduction   87
Mental Health Status of Rural Populations   88
Elderly Mental Disorders and Residence   90
Life Satisfaction of the Rural Elderly   91
Mental Health Services for the Rural Elderly   94
Research Needs   95
Summary   97
References   98

7 Housing and Transportation   103

Introduction   103
Home Ownership   104
Housing Quality   106
Housing Satisfaction   109
Housing Programs   109
Transportation   111
Transportation Availability   111
Transportation Adequacy   113
Transportation Programs   115
Research Needs   115
Summary   117
References   118

8 Informal Support: Family, Friends, and
      Neighbors   123

Introduction   123
Marital Status and Children   124
Contact with Children   126
Contact with Siblings   128
Nature of Support   128
Contact and Assistance from Friends and
      Neighbors   130
Research Needs   132

x   Contents

Summary   135
References   137

9 Formal Services and Service Provision   143

Introduction   143
Service Availability   144
The Rural Service Disadvantage   146
Service Accessibility   149
Service Utilization   149
   Attitudes Toward Service Use   151
   Service Awareness   152
Other Factors Related to Service Utilization   153
Problems in the Delivery of Services   155
Providing Services in Rural Settings   156
Research Needs   157
Summary   160
References   162

10 Summary and Concluding Remarks   167

Some Summary Observations   167
Confronting the Challenge: Policy and Planning   170
Concluding Remarks   173
References   175

Index   177

TABLES

2.1 Total Population and Population Aged 65 and
Over for Rural/Urban and Metropolitan/
Nonmetropolitan Areas of the United States, 1980   17

2.2 Total Population and Population Aged 65 and
Over for Rural/Urban and Metropolitan/
Nonmetropolitan Areas for Census Regions of the
United States, 1980   20

2.3 Number and Percentage Distribution of the White
and Black Population Aged 65 and Over for Rural/
Urban and Metropolitan/Nonmetropolitan Areas
of the United States, 1980   23

2.4 Number and Percentage Distribution of the Male
and Female Population Aged 65 and Over and Sex
Ratios of the Elderly for Rural/Urban and
Metropolitan/Nonmetropolitan Areas of the
United States, 1980   25

3.1 Percentage of Elderly Living In Families or Living
Alone with Incomes Below the Poverty Level for
Nonmetropolitan and Metropolitan Areas, 1979   42

PREFACE

My annotated bibliography published in 1983 stated that the existing literature on the rural elderly should be assessed and integrated before more research on this topic was undertaken. This book represents one attempt at such an assessment and integration. The literature on the rural elderly has increased considerably in both volume and scope since the publication of E. Grant Youmans' now classic collection, *Older Rural Americans: A Sociological Perspective* (University of Kentucky Press, 1967) and attests to the increased gerontological interest in this topic. Thus, the need for a careful review of what is known and not known about the life circumstances and problems of the rural elderly has grown both more imperative and more difficult.

As the studies and findings have multiplied, it has become evident to most gerontological observers of the rural scene that a considerable amount of variation characterizes the rural elderly. It has also been noted by many that the rural elderly, compared to the urban elderly, are disadvantaged in areas such as income, health, transportation, and housing, and, at the same time, have fewer formal services and resources available to them to meet these needs. Thus, some attention has begun to be focused on policy and program issues related to the provision of services to the rural elderly.

However, since much of the research on the rural elderly has been descriptive and non-comparative, few supportable gener-

alizations have emerged from these works. The studies themselves are found in a wide range of publications, reports, and
papers, and so on, further inhibiting the development of a coh-
erent and integrated body of knowledge. The purpose of this
book, then, is to bring together as much of the literature on the
rural elderly as possible and examine very basic questions concerning their status and needs and society's response to these
needs. It also lays out an agenda for future research by identifying those questions still in need of resolution that are central
to a more comprehensive and refined understanding of the rural
elderly. The book is intended for use by professional gerontologists, researchers, and practitioners alike, as well as by upper
level undergraduate and graduate students.

It is most likely that I have inadvertently excluded some research on the rural elderly and I apologize to those who feel
their contributions on this topic may have been overlooked.
Unfortunately, such oversights are almost inevitable in a work
of this nature. Finally, the presentation of the findings of others
is my responsibility alone and any inaccuracies in this regard
are both unintentional and regretted.

ACKNOWLEDGMENTS

While this book was for the most part written over a 12–month period, much of the reading, research, and thought that went into its making has spanned the better part of five years. Thus, while a number of individuals deserve acknowledgment for their efforts in direct support of this particular work, many others too numerous to mention have provided me with encouragement, advice, and insight as I have tried to come to terms with the many issues that affect the rural elderly. I am grateful to them all and hope they feel some satisfaction as they read the following pages.

I am also grateful to the staff of Greenwood Press, who have worked to see this project completed in a professional and timely manner, and to the State University of New York, College at Fredonia, for their support of my research. A special appreciation is expressed to the American Association of Retired Persons' Andrus Foundation for its support of several of my studies of topics related to the rural elderly. This support was instrumental in the development of my work on the rural elderly.

Special thanks and recognition go to two individuals for their assistance in this project. Mrs. Marlene Chizmadia typed (and re-typed) more drafts of this work than I care to admit to having written. Her professionalism, hard work, and good cheer were ever constant. Finally, my spouse, Bobbi Krout, was always there to listen to my musings and rumblings and was a never flagging source of support and encouragement. There are really no words adequate to express my appreciation, so I will just say "thank you." This book is dedicated to her and to my stepson, Thomas Tutmaher.

1 INTRODUCTION

GOAL OF BOOK

The purpose of this book is to document and analyze the status and experiences of the elderly living in rural environments and to investigate how they compare to those elderly living in more urbanized settings. Despite a very large increase in the degree of scholarly and governmental interest in the status of older Americans, relatively little is currently known about the specific circumstances of the rural elderly, how they deal with problematic aspects of their daily lives, and how they may differ from the urban elderly on both accounts. As Coward (1979, 275) recently noted, although some 34,000 publications focusing on the elderly appeared between 1960 and 1978, "the amount of research on the rural elderly is meager when compared to that which is available on the aged who reside in urban settings." This tendency to ignore the rural elderly reflects a general orientation to the study of aging that overlooks the variability found within and between the aged populations in urban and rural areas and instead focuses on those aspects that set the aged, as a group, apart from the rest of society. And while an annotated bibliography of social science research on the rural elderly recently published by the author (Krout, 1983) indicates that the amount of this research has increased in the past five years, the available literature is found in diverse sources and has not been systematically integrated.

The goal of this work, then, is to bring together, review and critique, and draw appropriate generalizations from the existing literature on the rural elderly. The available research from major substantive areas will be analyzed to determine if, how, and why the status of being old in rural areas differs from other residential environments. Thus, the demographic, environmental, social, economic, and cultural characteristics of rural places and their impact on the rural elderly will be examined.

The need to focus more specifically on the rural elderly is manifest. While the majority of the elderly now live in metropolitan places and will probably continue to do so, it is nonmetropolitan areas that have a proportionally greater percentage of their population over age 65 (Zuiches and Brown, 1978). In addition, the movement of elderly to rural areas has been one of the most significant components of the surprising post–1970 nonmetropolitan turnaround from net out- to net in-migration (Beale, 1975, 1976).

These demographic facts are not without significance for questions of service planning and provision. Not only do rural areas have a proportionally larger elderly target population, but the number of potential service recipients is increasing. Such increases may lead to additional strains on rural support networks in the future. Without a better understanding of the needs of the rural elderly and how they are met, professionals working in the service provision field will be handicapped in their efforts to design and implement effective service strategies. Thus, a work such as this is not only needed to further our knowledge of the rural elderly per se but is also relevant for questions of policy, program planning, and resource allocation.

DEFINITION OF "RURAL"

While the exact meaning and importance of the term "rural" has been debated countless times, the term most commonly is used to refer to three dimensions: ecological, occupational, and socio-cultural (Bealer et al., 1965). Researchers studying rural phenomena have generally relied on indicators of the first dimension (ecological) for classification purposes. The ecological dimension refers to the size, density, and location of a population vis-à-vis other population units, with population size almost always used as the sole criterion for rural/urban differentiation. Small population size and relative isolation can be expected to result in social and cultural differences from urban areas, and thus ecological variations are seen as most appropriate for defining rurality. Even though rural/urban should be viewed as a continuum, the practice historically has been to select a population size figure that separates the rural from the nonrural. In 1910, the U.S. Census Bureau used 2,500 for this purpose but in 1930 added the rural farm/rural nonfarm differentiation. More recently, a metropolitan/nonmetropolitan distinction has become commonplace (Adams, 1975). "Nonmetropolitan" refers to any county that is not part of a standard metropolitan statistical area (SMSA) and therefore includes rural farm, rural nonfarm, and towns and cities all the way up to 50,000 in population.

Unfortunately, many authors do not clearly indicate the population criteria they are using in discussions of the rural elderly. The term "nonmetropolitan" can be especially problematic because a wide diversity of residential environments are found in such areas (Coward, 1979; Lawton, 1977). In the present study, the term "rural" will refer to settings outside of cities of at least 50,000 and their suburbs (essentially the Census Bureau's definition of "nonmetropolitan"). However, this work explicitly acknowledges the actual continuum of living environments that ranges from rural farm to metropolitan central city.

RURAL/URBAN DIFFERENCES

One of the most profound and frequently analyzed changes in recent Western history has been the transformation of society from a rural/agrarian economic and social structure to a highly urban/industrial one. Classical sociologists such as Tonnies (1963) argued that urbanization occurred concomitantly with significant changes in culture and values, social interaction, individual behavior, and political, economic, and social organization. Rural areas, with their labor-intensive economies based on agriculture and resource extraction, were characterized as stable, homogeneous, less complex organizationally, and oriented to the community and primary group relations. Cities, on the other hand, were seen as characterized by rapid social change, heterogeneity, complex organizations, orientation to individuality, and secondary group social interaction.

More contemporary social scientists such as Wirth (1936) and Milgrim (1970) have argued that the sheer population size and density of the modern metropolis have triggered adaptations in the social interaction patterns of its inhabitants. City residents are seen as less friendly, more defensive, and less likely to become involved in the problems of others. Yet other social scientists (Fischer, 1976; Gans, 1962) have argued that rural/urban differences cannot be attributed to population size and density alone.

Values

It has been noted that both classical and contemporary thinkers have argued the predominant value system of rural areas is different in degree, if not kind, from that found in urban places. The term "values" refers to the goals, desired states, or shared criteria used by people to guide and judge the actions of others and the circumstances around them. Although not limited to rural areas, the following values have been identified as particularly important to the lives of rural people: practicality, efficiency, work, friendliness, honesty, patriotism, deep religious commitment, social conservatism, and a mistrust of government (Ford, 1962; Williams, 1970). These values are seen as resulting from the combined effects of geographic isolation, sparse population density, dominance of agriculture, ethnic homogeneity, and low geographic mobility (Christensen, 1981).

It has been argued that changes in the economies of rural areas and the spread of modern communication technologies have resulted in the replacement of a distinctive rural culture by a "mass" society. As a result, some authors note that few significant differences should be expected between rural and urban attitudes, behaviors, and values (Glenn and Hill, 1977; Pihlblad, 1975). However, just because rural society in America has changed socially and economically does not mean that its distinctive value structure has disappeared. A number of studies have concluded that important differences in values still exist between rural and urban populations (Larson, 1978; Lowe and Peek, 1974; Schnore, 1966; Willits et al., 1982). Even so, it should be added that the strength of rural/urban differences may not be great (Hassinger, 1978) and that there is considerable diversity in the value structure of rural America (Larson, 1978).

The debate about whether or not rural/urban differences in values still exist and their importance in explaining other phenomena is likely to continue for quite some time. No claim is made here as to what the correct outcome of this debate should be. In any event, several sociologists (Rose, 1967) have noted that the central fact in regard to rural/urban differences among the elderly is not rural/urban differences in 1985 but the differences that existed in the early 1900's, when the present-day cohort of elderly was socialized.

Much of the gerontological literature would appear to adhere to the traditional view of rural/urban differences and to assume that these differences exist unless proven otherwise. It is suggested here that this is much too simplistic a position. Indeed, rural and urban environments have many common characteristics. But there are no doubt differences between the rural and urban elderly in basic values and life style (Auerbach, 1976; White, 1977), and these differences, along with differences in needs and resources, must be taken into consideration when planning supportive services in rural areas (Windley, 1975). However, the degree, nature, and antecedents of these differences have not been adequately investigated and constitute a major area of future research. It is hoped that this book will help formulate these important research questions by bringing the existing literature into clearer focus.

Physical Differences

Much attention is given in the literature to an examination of rural/urban differences in terms of social and economic organization, values and attitudes, and behavior. Often, however, the very obvious physical differences of such places are overlooked. Small-town and farm areas do have significant physical contrasts with more urbanized areas—especially metropolitan central cities. As Rowles (1984) notes, rural places are more natural environments, with more vegetation and open space. In metropolises, generally 20 percent of the land is used for roads and highways, 30 percent for residences, and 13 percent for manufacturing or commercial structures. Rowles (1984,132) argues that the physical characteristics of rural settings present "lower levels of cognitive complexity and stimulus input" and change gradually.

SOME GUIDING OBSERVATIONS

This book is eclectic in that it draws on the work of a broad range of social scientists and others. The aim here is not to argue that the rural elderly are one thing or the other. At the same time, the author believes that a number of fundamental observations should be kept in mind as the reader works his or her way through the various research findings and arguments concerning the status of older rural Americans presented in this book.

Variability Among the Rural Elderly

A number of writers have argued the available research indicates that a considerable amount of variation exists between rural places and among the elderly living there (Coward, 1979; Krout, 1984; Lee and Lassey, 1980a). There is a tendency for gerontologists and others to use the words "rural" and "urban" as if they represented a neat dichotomy descriptive of two very distinct and different environments. It is the position of this author that such a perspective often results in the incomplete, inaccurate, and misleading collection and analysis of data. There is a great deal of diversity within and between living environments subsumed under the term "rural"—open country farm and nonfarm, small villages and towns, small cities, and the outlying areas of larger cities.

Thus, any examination of rural elderly must take that variability into account and acknowledge that differences largely associated with population size and density can be magnified by other geographic and socio-demographic factors. Caution must therefore be exercised in generalizing from studies that do not take account of this variability. And while parsimony requires that the term "rural" be used throughout this work, the reader should keep in mind the limitations associated with the use of such a term. In reality, the elderly live (as do others) in a continuum of residential environments. The central questions are if and how the ecological characteristics of less populated, lower density areas and the economic, social, and cultural systems associated with them differ significantly from more densely populated places and how these differences affect the elderly.

Disadvantaged Status of the Rural Elderly

While many Americans have an idealized view of the open country as being clean, crime-free, and less hectic than the big city, it is also generally recognized that rural areas are characterized by greater poverty, less adequate housing and transportation, and a lack of availability and accessibility of a wide range of services when compared to urban places. A sizeable amount of the gerontological literature has suggested that the rural elderly are disadvantaged on these factors and therefore have more unmet needs than the urban elderly. Older rural Americans, it is argued, have less income (Auerbach, 1976; Coward, 1979; Kim, 1981; Schooler, 1975), poorer health (Ellenbogen, 1967; Schooler, 1975; Youmans, 1967, 1974, 1977), and inferior housing (Coward, 1979; Montgomery, 1967) and have access to less adequate transportation systems (Cottrell, 1971; Harris, 1978; Patton, 1975). In fact, it has been stated that the rural elderly face a double jeopardy, suffering the disadvantages of being both old and rural (New York State Senate, 1980).

However, as will be seen throughout the course of this book, precious little comparative research has been conducted to identify if and how objective status measures differ between the rural and urban elderly and whether these differences are reflected in levels of satisfaction and service demand and utilization behavior. In fact, the author would argue that while there are indeed some status differences based on residence, not all the research supports the proposition that the rural aged are significantly worse off than their big-city counterparts. Thus, the question of the relative disadvantaged status of the rural versus urban elderly has not been adequately resolved. The degree, nature, and meaning of differences on objective measures of well-being will be systematically examined in this book.

Rural Elderly Needs Assessment Literature

Closely related to this issue is the question of how one determines whether or not a need exists. A need can be defined as a gap between what is viewed as a necessary level or condition and the objective status of an individual or group (Ecosometrics, 1981). Thus, to determine if there is a need, one must first know the desired state of affairs (goal) and decide if and how the actual state of affairs relates to it. To do this, empirical measures of both must be available and some framework must be applied to determine when a discrepancy exists between the two. A comprehensive review of the literature on the rural elderly has concluded that the rural elderly needs assessment literature is characterized by "serious conceptual weaknesses and operational deficiencies that raise considerable doubt as to the validity of past research and its generalizations" (Ecosometrics, 1981, 122). The following points serve as a basis for this conclusion: the absence of any generically defined and prioritized social welfare goals for the rural elderly; inconsistent geographic definitions of "rural" found in the literature; failure to identify uniquely rural factors underlying the needs of the rural elderly; conceptual and operational problems of judging rural elderly needs in reference to an urban standard; and the failure to recognize the considerable population and territorial diversity of rural America. These and other concerns underscore the need to be ever so cautious in interpreting research findings and generalizing from existing studies.

Life Satisfaction of the Rural Elderly

A number of studies (Hynson, 1975; Krout and Larson, 1980; Lee and Lassey, 1980b) have documented that whatever differences exist based on standard needs assessments, the rural el-

derly do not see their life or circumstances as particularly problematic. In fact, many researchers report finding high morale
and life satisfaction for elderly populations living in diverse settings (Donnenwerth et al., 1978; Grams and Fingler, 1981; Hynson, 1975; Lee and Lassey, 1980a, b; Rowles, 1981).

While the significance of this finding is open to interpretation,
the author would suggest several meanings to it. First, as others
have suggested (Ansello, 1981), such a finding calls into question
the adequacy and appropriateness of traditional needs assessment methods for studies of the rural elderly. Second, it bears
on the significance of research indicating that the rural elderly
have more needs than the urban elderly. It leads one to ask,
"needs" as defined by whom? A condition does not become a
need unless it is defined as one and, further, does not directly
impinge on matters of service provision unless the "needy" individual and the social service system act to respond to it.

Third, if in fact the rural elderly are not as well off according
to standard measures of income, health, and so on, what extra-
neous variables can account for this apparent lack of impact of
the observed conditions? What roles do cultural values, alternative social arrangements, or other unrecognized (by the researcher) phenomena play in this apparent paradox? The point
here is that one should be careful not to automatically assume
that statistical comparisons indicating the rural elderly are worse
off than the urban elderly necessarily mean that life as experienced by the rural elderly is qualitatively or even quantitatively
inferior. Perhaps the statistical differences partly reflect the fact
that the life circumstances of the rural elderly are simply different.

ORGANIZATION OF BOOK

This book covers a number of the standard topics addressed
in the gerontological literature and pays particular attention to
the information available on rural/urban differences. Each chapter follows the same basic format and begins with a review of
the literature on the status of the rural elderly on a particular
topic, the degree and nature of rural/urban differences, and any
changes that may have occurred in these differences over time.
The important research questions on these topics and their im-

plications for the life experiences of the rural elderly are identified and the significance of the research findings for programs,
policies, and service provision are examined. Finally, each chapter has a section on the issues and problems that future research
should address, a chapter summary, and references.

REFERENCES

Adams, D.L. 1975, "Who Are the Rural Aged?" in *Rural Environment
and Aging*, R.C. Atchley and T.O. Byerts (eds.), Gerontological
Society, Washington, D.C.

Ansello, E.F. 1981, "Antecedent Principles in Rural Gerontology Education," in *Toward Mental Health of the Rural Elderly*, P. Kim and
C. Wilson (eds.), University Press of America, Washington, D.C.

Auerbach, A.J. 1976, "The Elderly in Rural Areas: Differences in Urban
Areas and Implications for Practice," in *Social Work in Rural Com-
munities. L.* Ginsberg (ed.), Council on Social Work Education,
New York.

Beale, C.L. 1975, *The Revival of Population Growth in Nonmetropolitan
America*, Economic Research Service, U.S. Department of Agriculture, U.S. Government Printing Office, Washington, D.C.

————. 1976, "A Further Look at Nonmetropolitan Population Growth
Since 1970," paper presented at the annual meeting of the Rural
Sociological Society, New York, August.

Bealer, R., F.K. Willits, and W.P. Kuvelsky. 1965, "The Meaning of
Rurality in American Society: Some Implications of Alternative
Definitions," *Rural Sociology*, 30, 255–256.

Christensen, J. 1981, "Value Configurations for Ruralites and Urbanites:
A Comment on Bealer's Paper," *The Rural Sociologist*, 1, 42–47.

Cottrell, F. 1971, *Transportation of Older People in a Rural Community*,
Scripps Foundation, Oxford, Ohio.

Coward, R.T. 1979, "Planning Community Services for the Rural Elderly: Implications from Research," *The Gerontologist*, 19, 275–
282.

Donnenwerth, G.V., G. Guy, and M.J. Norwell. 1978, "Life Satisfaction
Among Older Persons: Rural-Urban and Racial Comparisons,"
Social Service Quarterly, 59, 578–583.

Ecosometrics. 1981, *Review of Reported Differences Between the Rural and
Urban Elderly: Status, Needs, Services, and Service Costs*, final report
to the Administration on the Aging (Contract No. 105–80–C–
065), Washington, D.C.

Ellenbogen, B.L. 1967, "Health Status of the Rural Aged," in *Older*

Rural Americans: A Sociological Perspective, E. Youmans (ed.), University of Kentucky Press, Lexington, Kentucky.

Fischer, C. 1976, *The Urban Experience*, Harcourt, Brace, Jovanovich, New York.

Ford, T. 1962, "The Passing of Provincialism," in *The Southern Appalachian Region: A Survey*, T. Ford (ed.), University of Kentucky Press, Lexington, Kentucky.

Gans, H. 1962, "Urbanism and Suburbanism as Ways of Life: A Reevaluation of Definitions," in *Human Behavior and Social Processes*, A. Rose (ed.), Houghton Miffin, Boston.

Glenn, N.D., and L. Hill. 1977, "Rural-Urban Differences in Attitudes and Behavior in the United States," *Annals of the American Academy of Political and Social Sciences*, 429, 36–50.

Grams, A., and A.P. Fengler. 1981, "Vermont Elders: No Sense of Deprivation," *Perspective on Aging*, 10, 12–15.

Harris, C.S. 1978, *Fact Book on Aging, A Profile of Americas's Older Population*, National Council on the Aging, Washington, D.C.

Hassinger, E. 1978, *The Rural Component of American Society*, Inter-State Printers and Publishers, Danville, Illinois.

Hynson, L.M. 1975, "Rural-Urban Differences in Satisfaction Among the Elderly," *Rural Sociology*, 40, 64–65.

Kim, P.K. 1981, "The Low Income Rural Elderly: Under-Served Victims of Public Inequity," in *Toward Mental Health of the Rural Elderly*, P.K. Kim and C. Wilson (eds.), University Press of America, Washington, D.C.

Krout, J.A. 1983, *The Rural Elderly: An Annotated Bibliography of Social Science Research*, Greenwood Press, Westport, Connecticut.

———. 1984, *The Utilization of Formal and Informal Support of the Aged: Rural Versus Urban Differences*, Final report to the American Association of Retired Persons, Andrus Foundation, Fredonia, New York.

Krout, J.A., and D. Larson. 1980, "Self-Assessed Needs of the Rural Elderly," paper presented at the annual meeting of the Rural Sociological Society, Ithaca, New York, August.

Larson, O. 1978, "Values and Beliefs of Rural People," in *Rural U.S.A.: Persistence and Change*, T. Ford (ed.), Iowa State University Press, Ames, Iowa.

Lawton, M. 1977, "The Impact of the Environment on Aging and Behavior," in *Handbook of the Psychology of Aging*, J. Birren and K. Schaie (eds.), Van Nostrand and Reinhold, New York.

Lee, G.R., and M.L. Lassey. 1980a, "Rural-Urban Differences Among the Elderly: Economic, Social and Subjective Factors," *Journal of Social Issues*, 36, 62–74.

————. 1980b, "Rural-Urban Residence and Aging: Directions for Future Research," in *Research and Public Service with the Elderly*, W. Lassey, M. Lassey, G. Lee, and N. Lee (eds.), Western Rural Development Center, Publication No. 4, Oregon State University, Corvallis, Oregon.

Lowe, G., and C. Peek. 1974, "Location and Lifestyle: The Comparative Explanatory Ability of Urbanism and Rurality," *Rural Sociology*, 39, 392–420.

Milgrim, S. 1970, "The Experience of Living in Cities," *Science*, 167, 1461–1468.

Montgomery, J.E., 1967, "Housing of the Rural Aged," in *Older Rural Americans*, E. Youmans (ed.), University of Kentucky Press, Lexington, Kentucky.

New York State Senate. 1980, *Old Age and Ruralism: A Case of Double Jeopardy, Report on the Rural Elderly*, New York State Senate, Albany, New York.

Patton, C.V. 1975, "Age Groupings and Travel in a Rural Area," *Rural Sociology*, 40, 55–63.

Pihlblad, C.T. 1975, "Culture, Life Style, and Social Environment of the Small Town," in *Rural Environments and Aging*, R. Atchley and T.O. Byerts (eds.), Gerontological Society, Washington, D.C.

Rose, A. 1967, "Perspectives on the Rural Aged," in *Older Rural Americans*, E.G. Youmans (ed.), University of Kentucky Press, Lexington, Kentucky.

Rowles, G.D. 1981, *The Geographical Experience of the Elderly, Final Progress Report*, Washington, D.C., National Institute on Aging, Grant AG00862.

————. 1984, "Aging in Rural Environments," in *Elderly People and the Environment*, J. Altman, M. Lawton, and J. Wohlwill (eds.), Plenum Press, New York.

Schnore, L. 1966, "The Rural-Urban Variable: An Urbanite's Perspective," *Rural Sociology*, 31, 131–143.

Schooler, K. 1975, "A Comparison of Rural and Non-Rural Elderly on Selected Variables," in *Rural Environments and Aging*, R. Atchley and T.O. Byerts (eds.), Gerontological Society, Washington, D.C.

Tonnies, F. 1963, *Community and Society*, C.P. Loomis (trans.), Harper, New York.

White, M.A. 1977, "Values of Elderly Differ in Rural Setting," *Generations*, Fall, 67.

Williams, R. 1970, *American Society*, Knopf, New York.

Willits, F., R. Bealer, and D. Crider. 1982, "Persistence of Rural/Urban Differences," in *Rural Society in the U.S.: Issues for the 1980's*, D.

Dillman and D. Hobbes (eds.), Westview Press, Boulder, Colorado.

Windley, P.G. 1975, "Reaction to Who Are the Rural Aged? by David Adams," in *Rural Environments and Aging*, R.C. Atchley and T.O. Byerts (eds.), Gerontological Society, Washington, D.C.

Wirth, L. 1936, "Urbanism as a Way of Life," *American Journal of Sociology*, 44, 3–24.

Youmans, E.G. 1967, "Health Orientations of Older Rural and Urban Men," *Geriatrics*, 22, 139–147.

———. 1974, "Age Groupings and Health Attitudes," *The Gerontologist*, 14, 249.

———. 1977, "The Rural Aged," *Annals of the American Academy of Political Science*, 429, 81–90.

Zuiches, J., and D. Brown. 1978, "The Changing Character of the Nonmetropolitan Population, 1970–1976," in *Rural U.S.A.: Persistence and Change*, T. Ford (ed.), Iowa State University Press, Ames, Iowa.

2 DEMOGRAPHIC CHARACTERISTICS

INTRODUCTION

Historically, the United States has seen itself as the country of the young, and for many years it has been. In 1900, only 3 million people, or 4 percent of the total population, were aged 65 or over. But by 1983, 26 million, or 11 percent of the populace, were elderly (Weeks, 1984), and projections indicate the number of elderly will rise to 32 million by the year 2000 and 55 million by 2030, with corresponding elderly percentages of the population hitting 12.2 and 18.3 respectively (Ward, 1984). In addition, the fastest growing segment of the population is the "old-old," 85 years and older (Soldo, 1980). The sheer size of this demographic shift and its personal, social, and economic implications have as much as anything brought national attention to the status and needs of the elderly. The causes of the elderly demographic explosion are many, but it resulted largely from the high fertility levels of the late 19th and 20th centuries and higher probabilities of survival due to improvements in medicine and sanitation (Clifford et al., 1985). The proportion of the total population that is elderly has increased largely due to lower fertility rates in the 20th century (Weeks, 1984).

The purpose of this chapter is to review the demographics of the elderly population residing in rural areas. Not only is it important to examine the numbers and proportions of elderly living in rural areas, it is also necessary to develop their socio-demographic profile. The status and needs of the rural elderly identified in the following chapters can be fully understood only in relationship to this population's characteristics. In addition, the variation that exists in the geographic distribution of the rural elderly and the recent changes that have affected it will be examined. A discussion of questions in need of further study and a summary section conclude this chapter.

HOW MANY RURAL ELDERLY?

As was noted in the introduction, the term "rural" is defined in many ways and a rural/urban distinction, even in a seemingly straightforward area such as population size, has not been consistently agreed upon or applied. In some ways, this is as it should be because "rural/urban" does represent a continuum of environments. However, this lack of specificity makes the collection, presentation, and analysis of data on the rural elderly difficult at best. The primary source of national-level population data, the U.S. Census Bureau, presents data on the elderly for a large number of community type designations.

Traditionally, the Census Bureau has classified as urban the populations of places with 2,500 or more inhabitants and the populations of urbanized areas. According to the 1980 census, "urbanized area" refers to any incorporated place and its densely populated surrounding area that has at least 50,000 inhabitants (Weeks, 1984). "Rural" exists as a residual category that covers any other population. Both urbanized area and rural categories are often broken down further. Unfortunately, these designations are not used consistently for all variables, thus complicating comparisons. Nonetheless, the census is an invaluable source of information and will be relied on heavily in this chapter.

The number of elderly that can be said to reside in rural areas depends, of course, on the definition one uses for "rural." Data presented in Table 2.1 come from the 1980 census and are broken down by both the traditional rural/urban and nonmetropolitan/metropolitan distinctions. Using the rural/urban designation, approximately 6.5 million persons aged 65 and over lived in rural areas in 1980 and 19 million lived in urban areas. The elderly

TABLE 2.1

Total Population and Population Aged 65 and Over for Rural/Urban and
Metropolitan/Nonmetropolitan Areas of the United States, 1980

Residence Areas	All Ages	Number 65 and Over	Percentage
TOTAL	226,546[a]	25,549	11.3
URBAN	167,051	19,046	11.4
Inside urbanized areas	139,171	15,158	10.9
Central cities	67,035	8,015	12.0
Urban fringe	72,136	7,182	10.0
Outside urbanized areas	27,880	3,848	13.8
10,000 plus	13,482	1,736	12.9
2,500 to 10,000	14,398	2,112	14.7
RURAL	59,495	6,503	10.9
1,000 to 2,500	7,038	1,085	15.4
Other	52,457	5,418	10.3
METROPOLITAN	169,431	18,080	10.7
NONMETROPOLITAN	57,115	7,424	13.0

[a]Numbers in thousands.

Source: 1980 Census of Population, Volume 1, Characteristics of the Population,
Chapter B, General Population Characteristics, Part 1, United States
Summary, Table 43, Bureau of the Census, May, 1983.

accounted for a smaller proportion of the total population in
rural than urban places—10.9 and 11.4 percent respectively. These
figures indicate a change from prior decades, when the elderly
made up a slightly higher percentage of the rural populace (10.1

versus 9.8 for rural and urban respectively in 1970) (Clifford et al., 1985).

The data in Table 2.1 indicate that the highest percentage of an area's population that is elderly (15.4) is found for small towns in rural areas. The lowest percentage (10.0) is found for the urban fringe or suburban areas of urbanized territory. The former is likely due to a combination of the out-migration of young adults and the relative lack of mobility of the elderly and movement of retired farmers (and their spouses) into nearby small towns (Siegel, 1979). The latter is probably a result of the preference that families with small children have for suburban places, the relatively high cost of housing in suburban areas, and residential/commercial patterns that require a high degree of physical mobility (i.e., stores are usually concentrated in shopping malls and not close to residences). Some observers have argued that this youthful out-migration has important implications for the well-being of the elderly, leaving them with fewer social contacts and a restricted social support system (Diemling and Huber, 1981).

The data in Table 2.1 also indicate that a negative correlation exists between population size and the proportion of the population aged 65 and over. While this proportion is 15.4 percent for rural places of from 1,000 to 2,500, it declines to 14.7 and 12.9 percent respectively for places of 2,500 to 10,000 and 10,000 and over outside urbanized areas. The percentage for places within urbanized areas is 10.9. Data from the 1980 census not shown here indicate that slightly more than 700,000 elderly live on what are classified as rural farms (less than 3 percent of the elderly population). The elderly made up 12.7 percent of that total rural farm population. It is likely that this rural farm elderly percentage is lower than the rural 1,000-to-2,500 percentage because of the tendency of farmers, especially widows, to move off farms to nearby small towns as they get older.

The somewhat problematic nature of rural/urban population comparisons is revealed when one looks at the figures in Table 2.1 for the metropolitan/nonmetropolitan designation. Here "metropolitan" refers to all the population contained within the boundaries of a metropolitan area or an SMSA—a central city of 50,000 or more and the surrounding counties judged to be economically and socially integrated with it. "Nonmetropolitan" refers to any county not part of a metropolitan area. Thus, the metropolitan/nonmetropolitan distinction uses counties as a basic unit for data presentation purposes.

Data in Table 2.1 indicate that when the metropolitan/non-metropolitan distinction is used as an indicator of rurality, the number of rural elderly increases to 7.4 million (up almost one million) and the proportion of the rural population that is elderly grows from 10.9 to 13 percent. This is considerably greater than the 10.7 percent registered for metropolitan areas. In fact, the proportion of elderly increases when partly urban nonmetro-politan counties are examined separately from all rural non-metropolitan counties (12.8 and 14.3 percent respectively). It is also important to note that the higher proportion of population aged 65 and over found for the nonmetropolitan designation exists for every census region, every census division (except the Pacific), and all but eleven states (Arizona, Colorado, Florida, Louisiana, Maryland, Nevada, Oregon, Rhode Island, Tennes-see, Vermont, and West Virginia).

The number and proportion of elderly people that can be classified as rural, then, does depend on the particular definition in use. Regardless of the definition, however, the proportion of an area's population that is elderly generally increases as pop-ulation size decreases. This means that the dependency ratio (the ratio of elderly to those in the so-called productive years of 18–64) is larger for these more rural places. This may place an added burden on the ability of the economies of such places to support programs and services for the elderly. At the same time, higher percentages of elderly may mean larger reference groups for rural elders.

GEOGRAPHIC DISTRIBUTION

Data presented in Table 2.2 show the number of elderly in each of the nation's four census regions for both metropolitan and nonmetropolitan counties for 1980. As would be expected, the absolute number of elderly is greater in metropolitan as opposed to nonmetropolitan areas. But for every census region, the proportion of the total population that is aged 65 or over is greater in nonmetropolitan versus metropolitan areas. The North

TABLE 2.2

Total Population and Population Aged 65 and Over for Rural/Urban and Metropolitan/Nonmetropolitan Areas for Census Regions of the United States, 1980

Residence Area	Northeast	Region North Central	South	West
INSIDE METROPOLITAN AREAS				
Total all ages	41,792[a]	41,713	50,367	35,609
Total 65 and over	5,093	4,271	5,267	3,494
Percent 65 and over	12.2	12.7	10.5	12.2
URBAN				
Total	4,565	3,705	4,468	3,223
Central city	2,192	1,952	2,367	1,551
Not in central city	2,373	1,753	2,101	1,671
RURAL	529	565	799	271
OUTSIDE METROPOLITAN AREAS				
Total all ages	7,393	17,152	25,005	7,564
Total 65 and over	978	2,421	3,221	804
Percent 65 and over	13.2	17.0	12.9	13.2
Urban	420	1,005	1,250	409
Rural	558	1,416	1,971	395

[a]Number in thousands.

Source: 1980 Census of Population, Volume 1, Characteristics of the Population, Chapter B, General Population Characteristics, Part 1, United States Summary, Table 55, Bureau of the Census, May, 1983.

Central region has by far the highest percentage of elderly (17 percent), while the other three regions are very close to the nonmetropolitan average of 13 percent.

Data not presented in Table 2.2 indicate that the North Central region also has the highest proportion of population aged 65 and over in partly urban nonmetropolitan counties (13.7 percent), followed by the Northeast (13.4 percent), South (12.8 percent), and West (9.8 percent). A similar trend is found for percentages of elderly in all rural nonmetropolitan counties: North Central, 17.1 percent; Northeast, 14.9 percent; South, 13.2 percent; and West, 10.6 percent.

It should be noted that the data in Table 2.2 show that the South has the largest *number* of nonmetropolitan (and metropolitan) elderly. In fact, 43.4 percent of the nonmetropolitan elderly live in the South and 32.6 percent live in the North Central region. The South and North Central regions are more rural (in terms of total population distribution) than are the other areas. Only 13.2 percent of the nonmetropolitan elderly reside in the highly urbanized Northeast and 10.8 percent in the more sparsely populated West. Thus, fully three-quarters of the nonmetropolitan elderly live in two of the four geographic regions of the country.

Of course, there is considerable variation within regions and at the local level on the percentage of the population that is elderly. The states with the highest percentage of totally rural area populations aged 65 and over in 1980 were Kansas, Iowa, Massachusetts, Missouri, and Nebraska (all 18 percent or more). The states with the lowest proportions of elderly in rural counties were Alaska, Colorado, Louisiana, Maryland, Nevada, and New Mexico (4.1 to 9.6 percent) (Clifford et al., 1985). Another important demographic observation is that for many more states, significant percentages of the state's elderly population live in rural areas. A majority of the elderly in 21 states live in rural areas (Kim, 1981), and two-fifths of the elderly population is rural in 28 states (Harbert and Wilkinson, 1979).

Thus, the concentrations of rural elderly found across the nation vary widely between regions and especially states. These differences generally result from variations in fertility and migration trends, with areas showing high concentrations of elderly usually having experienced moderate levels of fertility and steady out-migration throughout this century (Clifford et al., 1985). These demographic differences mean that some states have large numbers and/or percentages of rural elderly while others do not. Consequently, the relative visibility and importance of the rural elderly as a special popluation and local responses to them can be expected to vary widely.

SOCIO-DEMOGRAPHIC CHARACTERISTICS

A number of differences are found between the rural and urban elderly in basic socio-demographic characteristics. This section will compare the rural and urban elderly in terms of race, sex composition, and marital and family status.

Racial Differences

In terms of racial background, the large majority of white, black, and "other" elderly reside in urban areas. Data presented in Table 2.3, however, show that a greater percentage of white than black elderly are found in rural places (26.2 percent for whites versus 19.4 percent for blacks). Concomitantly, a greater percentage of black elderly reside in urban areas, especially in urbanized areas (68.1 percent for black versus 58.4 percent for whites). Over 55 percent of all black elderly live in central cities and only 12.5 percent live in the urban fringe, while comparable percentages for whites are 28.7 and 29.7. This pattern of residential location by race for the elderly corresponds to the pattern for the population as a whole.

Several other statistics on nonmetropolitan/metropolitan differences in the racial background of the elderly not presented in Table 2.3 are also of interest. First of all, the black elderly make up a much larger percentage of the total metropolitan as opposed to nonmetropolitan population (2.7 versus 0.9 percent). Second, a smaller percentage of the nonmetropolitan as opposed to metropolitan elderly are black (7.3 versus 8.8 percent). Thus, blacks make up a smaller percentage of the overall nonmetropolitan population and the nonmetropolitan elderly population.

TABLE 2.3

Number and Percentage Distribution of the White and Black Population
Aged 65 and Over for Rural/Urban and Metropolitan/Nonmetropolitan Areas
of the United States, 1980

| | White 65 and Over | | Black 65 and Over | |
	Number	Percent	Number	Percent
TOTAL	22,948[a]		2,087	
URBAN	16,933	73.8	1,682	80.6
Inside Urban Areas	13,405	58.4	1,421	68.1
Central cities	6,597	28.7	1,160	55.6
Urban Fringe	6,807	29.7	261	12.5
Outside Urban Areas	3,528	15.4	262	12.5
10,000 plus	1,576	6.9	131	6.2
2,500 to 10,000	1,952	8.5	131	6.2
RURAL	6,015	26.2	405	19.4
1,000 to 2,500	1,020	4.4	51	2.4
Other	4,995	21.8	354	16.7
METROPOLITAN	16,159	70.4	1,551	74.3
NONMETROPOLITAN	6,789	29.6	536	25.7

[a]Numbers in thousands.

Source: 1980 Census of Population, Volume 1, Characteristics of the Population,
Chapter B, General Population Characteristics, Part 1, United States
Summary, Table 43, Bureau of the Census, May, 1983.

Sex Differences

In terms of sex status, women predominate among the elderly in general. In 1980, six of every ten older Americans were female, and females outnumbered males by almost five million (Weeks, 1984). A common statistic used to express this balance (or imbalance) is the sex ratio—the number of males per 100 females. In 1980, the sex ratio was 68 (Weeks, 1984). As can be seen from data in Table 2.4, a sex ratio in favor of females exists for every residence category. The sex ratio differences within the urban categories are relatively small, but the ratio is much higher for rural areas as a whole (82.6 for rural versus 63.0 for urban). Within the rural category, it is evident that the higher ratio for the rural "other" category is largely responsible for the overall rural/urban difference.

Although less pronounced, there is also a sex ratio difference for metropolitan versus nonmetropolitan areas. These sex ratios indicate that elderly females are less likely to reside in rural or nonmetropolitan areas and that the opposite is true for males. Likewise, males make up a larger percentage of the rural/nonmetropolitan elderly than of the urban/metropolitan elderly. This difference is largely a consequence of sex-specific migration patterns in which elderly widows often move from farms to nearby small towns and villages whereas elderly widowers are more likely to stay on the farm. These sex ratio differences are important because of their predictable impacts on the marital status and living arrangements of rural versus urban elderly. Elderly females are more likely than males to be widowed and live alone, and it can be expected that rural areas will have greater proportions of their elderly experiencing such situations.

Marital Status Differences

Published 1980 census data on marital status differences for the elderly broken down by residence are only available using the nonmetropolitan/metropolitan distinction. The nonmetropolitan category is further broken down into the farm and nonfarm categories for greater specificity. Because sex is strongly related to marital status, the data are discussed for males and

TABLE 2.4

Number and Percentage Distribution of the Male and Female Population
Aged 65 and Over and Sex Ratios of the Elderly for Rural/Urban and
Metropolitan/Nonmetropolitan Areas of the United States, 1980

| | Male 65 and Over | | Female 65 and Over | | Elderly |
	Number	Percent	Number	Percent	Sex Ratio
TOTAL	10,305	100	15,244	100	67.6
URBAN	7,364	71.5	11,682	76.6	63.0
Inside Urbanized	5,896	57.2	9,299	61.0	63.4
Central cities	3,034	29.4	4,981	32.7	60.9
Urban fringe	2,864	27.8	4,318	28.3	66.3
Outside Urbanized	1,460	14.2	2,383	15.6	61.3
10,000 plus	652	6.3	1,084	7.1	60.0
2,500 to 10,000	813	7.9	1,299	8.5	62.6
RURAL	2,941	28.5	3,562	23.4	82.6
1,000 to 2,500	432	4.2	653	4.3	66.1
Other	2,509	24.3	2,909	19.1	86.3
METROPOLITAN	7,173	69.6	10,952	71.8	65.5
NONMETROPOLITAN	3,132	30.4	4,293	28.2	73.0

aNumbers in thousands.

Source: 1980 Census of Population, Volume 1, Characteristics of the Population,
Chapter B, General Population Characteristics, Part 1, United States
Summary, Table 43, Bureau of the Census, May, 1983.

females separately. These data show that the nonmetropolitan
elderly and especially farm dwellers are more likely to be married, both overall and for males and females. For every residence
category, males are twice as likely to be married as females,
while females are much more likely to be widowed. Nonmet-

ropolitan farm and nonfarm differences do emerge here for females. In farm areas only, 28.5 percent of elderly women are widowed, versus 51.8 percent for nonfarm areas. This reflects the tendency noted earlier of elderly widows to move off of farms. In addition, the nonmetropolitan female elderly, especially farm dwellers, are less likely to be divorced or separated, while nonmetropolitan farm males are much more likely to have been never married then either nonfarm males or nonfarm, farm, and metropolitan females.

Thus, nonmetropolitan areas (especially farm areas) are more likely to have elderly populations that are married and not widowed—a difference that is particularly strong for women. Since spouses are generally the first line of support for the elderly in need of personal care, these data suggest (at least on the surface) a nonmetropolitan and farm advantage. In addition, since married persons almost always live together, one would expect to find nonmetropolitan elderly (especially farm dwellers) less likely to be living alone—a situation often seen as placing the elderly at greater physical and psychological risk.

Family Status Differences

In general, it is known that aged males are much more likely to live in husband-wife family settings and much less likely to live alone than females (Weeks, 1984). Data from the 1980 Current Population Survey show that this is the case for every residence category. Women, because of their greater likelihood of widowhood, are more likely to live in other family settings than men (except in farm areas) and are much more likely to be living alone. Again, metropolitan/nonmetropolitan differences are forthcoming. Elderly husband-wife families are more predominant in nonmetropolitan versus metropolitan areas. Nonmetropolitan farm males are less likely to be living alone and more likely to be living with other family than nonfarm or metropolitan males, while the largest proportion of females living with other females is found for metropolitan areas. These residence differences for males and females result from a combination of lower female mortality and probability of remarrying as well as the net movement of intact elderly marriage units to nonmetropolitan areas (Clifford et al., 1985).

TRENDS IN SIZE OF RURAL ELDERLY POPULATION

It was not until 1920 that a majority of the total U.S. population lived in places with 2,500 or more inhabitants. For the next several decades, rural areas held increasingly smaller percentages of the U.S. population but the absolute number of rural residents did not fluctuate. Natural increase was offset by out-migration to urban/metropolitan areas and, moreover, a predominantly rural farm population became a rural nonfarm population (Beale, 1978).

Between 1950 and 1970, the proportion of the nation's population that was nonmetropolitan decreased from 41 to 36 percent, but the absolute number increased from 61 to 72 million. Concomitantly, the metropolitan proportion increased and the number of people living there swelled from 89 to 130 million (Taeuber, 1972). During this time, important shifts occurred in the age composition of the nonmetropolitan population. While the 20–49 age group declined both absolutely and proportionately as a result of out-migration and lowered fertility rates of the 1930's and 1940's, the 65 and over age group expanded by 2.3 million persons and from 8.6 to 11.2 percent of the nonmetropolitan population (Zuiches and Brown, 1978). Growth in the elderly segment of the population between 1950 and 1970 was responsible for a large part of the total nonmetropolitan increase, much more so than was the case in metropolitan areas (Zuiches and Brown, 1978). In fact, since 1950 the growth rate of the elderly in nonmetropolitan places has consistently been higher than that of the non-elderly (Fuguitt and Tordella, 1980).

NONMETROPOLITAN POPULATION TURNAROUND

Since 1970, however, a dramatic shift has occurred in the growth and migration rates of nonmetropolitan versus metropolitan areas. During this decade, nonmetropolitan places actually grew faster than metropolitan ones and received proportionately more migrants than they sent—an unanticipated rural population turnaround (Beale, 1975; Beale and Fuguitt, 1978). This resurgence of growth was experienced by nonmetropolitan places far removed from metropolitan areas as well as those adjacent to them and thus was not a case of "urban spillover." Between 1970 and 1975, fully one-half of the total nonmetropopulation gain of 3.5 million came from a net in-migration (Johnson and Purdy, 1980). This startling change from nonmetropolitan net out- to net in-migration can be accounted for by changes in two migration streams. Not only did the number of migrants to nonmetropolitan places from metropolitan places increase by approximately 25 percent, but the rate of out-migration from nonmetropolitan places decreased (Tucker, 1976; Zuiches and Brown, 1978).

Between 1970 and 1980, the growth in the elderly segment of the population in both nonmetropolitan and metropolitan counties was two to three times greater than that of the total population. The percentage change in the total population was 11.4 percent (10.3 percent and 15.1 percent in metropolitan and nonmetropolitan areas respectively). The nationwide change for the elderly between 1970 and 1980 was 27.9 percent (28.1 percent and 27.4 percent in metropolitan and nonmetropolitan areas respectively). The percentage change for the elderly was greater in those nonmetropolitan places adjacent to metropolitan areas (Clifford et al., 1985). Thus, not only did nonmetropolitan areas become older, but the percentage of the total U.S. elderly population living in nonmetropolitan places increased.

It is important to note geographic variations in the pattern of 1970–1980 change in the percentage of the population aged 65 and over in rural areas. Nationwide, all rural nonmetropolitan counties experienced only an 8 percent gain, while part urban nonmetropolitan counties registered a 31.4 percent increase. At the state level, all rural counties with the highest 1980 proportion of elderly actually had the lowest rates of elderly population change between 1970 and 1980 (Clifford et al., 1985). It is evident that the highest rates of growth of elderly did not necessarily occur in places with the greatest numbers of elderly. And the numbers of elderly may be more important for the planning and provision of services than the percentage (Clifford et al., 1985). What were the demographic factors underlying this growth in the rural elderly population? First, one should keep in mind that the predominant demographic antecedent of the absolute growth of the rural elderly population is the aging-in-place of younger age cohorts (Golant, 1975, 1979). The sizeable amount of demographic research conducted on the post–1970 nonmetropolitan population turnaround indicates, however, that net migration gains were important to the growth of the number and percentage of older people as well (Fuguitt and Tordella, 1980; Golant, 1979). Lichter et al. (1981) demonstrate that between 1950 and 1975, elderly migration became an increasingly important component of absolute nonmetropolitan elderly population growth and less important in the growth of large metropolitan elderly populations. Between 1970 and 1975, net migration gains in the 65 and over age category accounted for about 30 percent of the absolute change in this age group.

In fact, elderly net migration gains in nonmetropolitan areas occurred in the 1950's and 1960's and were harbingers of later migration changes for these places (Fuguitt and Tordella, 1980; Lichter et al., 1981). Presumably they contributed to the post–1970 net in-migration gains in the under 65 age group as the increased economic demand of the elderly created job opportunities. These gains in elderly net in-migration occurred in all regions of the United States (Northeast, North Central, South, and West) (Fuguitt and Tordella, 1980). However, more detailed regional analysis shows that the rural boom in elderly net in-migration was more pronounced in some places than in others. The South (particularly Florida) and Southwest and areas with considerable recreation facilities (upper Great Lakes, Ozarks) were strong gainers, while other nonmetropolitan areas had little or no elderly net in-migration (Great Plains, central Midwest, Appalachia, New York State) (Biggar, 1980; Fuguitt and Tordella, 1980).

It should be noted that demographic processes of the under 65 population (particularly out-migration of the young during the 1950's and 1960's) also served to increase the percentage of the elderly in nonmetropolitan places (Clifford et al., 1983). At the same time, those people who moved into nonmetropolitan areas in the 1970's were older than those who moved out (Zuiches and Brown, 1978). In general, those individuals who moved to nonmetropolitan places had higher occupational status and education levels and were more likely to be white and female (Zuiches and Brown, 1978). They also had higher incomes and were less likely to be poor than the resident nonmetropolitan population.

Regardless of the *rates* of elderly in-migration, the actual numbers who moved between nonmetropolitan and metropolitan places are also of importance. The elderly as a group have lower rates of mobility than other age groups (Shaw, 1975), with over two-thirds of the mobile elderly moving within environmental types (Longino and Biggar, 1981). According to Golant (1979), between 1970 and 1975 5 percent of the migrant elderly moved from nonmetropolitan places to metropolitan and 12 percent moved in the opposite direction. Thus, the actual number of rural elderly in-migrants nationally is small (400,000 between 1960 and 1975) (Fuguitt and Tordella, 1980).

It is generally recognized that the elderly move for different reasons than the non-elderly. As they are not usually members of the labor force, the elderly are less likely to move to look for a job or because of job training or transfer (Serow, 1978). Changes in life cycle such as loss of spouse and retirement (Yu and Van Arsdol, 1977), a desire to be near relatives (Wiseman, 1979), and improved climate and recreation opportunities (Barsby and Cox, 1975; Krout, 1983) have been identified as likely precipitators of elderly migration. It has already been suggested that the last mentioned was a factor in the recent movement of elderly to rural areas. Several studies have shown that "quality of life" factors such as environmental and recreational conditions are identified by rural elderly in-migrants as reasons for their move (Cebula, 1974; Williams and Sofranko, 1979).

A number of case studies of rural places receiving considerable elderly in-migration during the 1970's also suggest that return migration to areas of previous residence or place of birth has been a factor (Koebernick and Beegle, 1977; Roseman, 1977; Sofranko, 1981). It has also been noted that rural areas near larger cities which have served as former vacation places or the location of second homes are also selected by the elderly because of their familiarity (Koebernick and Beegle, 1978; Roseman, 1977; Voss and Fuguitt, 1979).

CONSEQUENCES OF RURAL ELDERLY INCREASE

The growth of the rural elderly population both in numbers and as a proportion of the total population can be expected to have significant impacts on those places. This increase, regardless of its roots in aging-in-place or migration, has not occurred evenly in all rural places, and thus the nature and degree of its consequences have also varied. In particular, those areas identified earlier as having received considerable in-migration of elderly can be expected to be more likely to experience the kinds of impacts discussed below. This point also underscores the fact that while nationwide the migration of the elderly involves a relatively small number of people, its impact in certain places has been significant indeed (Ecosometrics, 1981).

Of course, one of the most fundamental impacts of elderly in-migration to rural areas is its contribution to overall population growth in these places. A number of studies (Beale, 1975; Beale and Fuguitt, 1978; McCarthy and Morrison, 1979) have reported a strong positive association between elderly in-migration and overall population growth. But the social, political, and economic arenas may be affected as well. For example, new elderly migrants move to rural areas because of environmental and recreational amenities and the relatively low cost of living. Thus, they may well oppose attempts by younger (or older) "natives" for economic development (Aday and Miles, 1982; Koebernick and Beegle, 1978). Schwarzweller (1979) argues that social integration may be a problem for the new residents because of their urban behavior, attitudes, and values. Recall that the rural elderly in-migrants are somewhat different from the indigenous elderly population (more likely to be younger, male, married, own a home, and have higher incomes) (Longino, 1980).

Aday and Miles (1982) argue that these exurbanites may bring a different set of expectations about social services. And what of the adequacy of existing services? Some authors have suggested that new migrants might put strains on rural service systems and even reduce the availability of services for longtime residents (Monahan and Greene, 1982; Schwarzweller, 1979). And whatever the service needs of new elderly migrants upon arrival, they will likely increase as the migrants age. Very little research is available to determine what, in fact, the impact of elderly in-migration has been on rural areas. Several studies have indicated that the medical services of nonmetropolitan places with (or near areas with) increases in the elderly are *not* over-burdened and can meet the demand (Heintz, 1976; Lee, 1980). This may be, of course, a result of the propensity of the elderly to migrate to places that do have adequate services or because the incoming elderly contribute positively to the economic base of their new communities and may even affect economies of scale in service provision (Heintz, 1976).

RESEARCH NEEDS

The data on rural/urban differences in the number, race and sex composition, marital status, and living arrangements of the elderly presented in this chapter provide a basic understanding of the demographic variation of the rural elderly. However, not enough is known about differences in these characterisitics at the local level. State level statistics hide local variations, and it is these variations that impact the planning and provision of services. Very little is understood about how these basic de-mographic chracteristics affect the circumstances of the rural versus urban elderly and their communities.

Perhaps the most dramatic demographic trend involving the elderly in rural areas has been their net migration gains in the 1960's and especially the 1970's. Growth in any age category due to migration is deserving of special attention because its impact on the community is so immediate. Increases in the number and proportion of elderly in rural communities magnify the impor-tance of traditional areas of research such as social and health needs assessment, and it is clear that more research must be directed toward determining how changes in the absolute and relative numbers of elderly in rural areas will affect those places. Will new problems result or will old ones be exacerbated, and how will this demographic change affect existing policies of resource allocation? Furthermore, the complexity of research questions increases with the recognition that elderly in-migrants have different socio-demographic characteristics and possibly different attitudes and values than longtime rural residents.

Lee and Lassey (1982) have identified four areas related to rural elderly in-migration on which a paucity of information currently exists and which pose significant research questions for the future. First, the social and economic characteristics of the elderly in-migrants (as well as their values and attitudes) need to be documented. On balance, what resources do the new migrants bring to rural areas, what are their needs for services, and what might these needs be as they age in place? Second, why have they moved to rural places? This information will provide insight into their expectations and thus help the receiving communities more effectively prepare for them and future elderly in-migrants. Such data will also help social scientists anticipate their behavior and assess the potential for change or conflict in these communities. Third, what are the consequences (cost and benefits) of this migration for the migrants themselves? How well will they adapt to their new surroundings, and will they desire to and be able to become integrated into their new communities?

Finally, what consequences will result for the receiving communities, and how well will they be able to absorb the elderly migrants? In particular, elderly migration changes the age structure very rapidly. Will this mean a significantly different demand for hospitals, recreational facilities, housing, and all types of social services? Will property values rise at the same time the proportion of the community in the labor force and paying full taxes declines? More detailed information on all of these questions is needed to help social scientists refine the models that have been developed to explain demographic and social stability and change in rural places and populations, and to assist communities and agencies in their planning for the provision of basic services to the elderly and non-elderly alike.

SUMMARY

This chapter has examined some basic demographic aspects of the rural elderly. While the large majority of elderly in the

United States live in metropolitan or urban areas, approximately one-quarter to one-third reside outside of such places (depending on the definition of rural that is used). Almost three-quarters of the rural elderly live in the South and North Central regions of the country.

Moreover, the proportion of a place's population that is 65 and over increases as population size decreases, leaving rural areas with higher concentrations of elderly persons. A consequence of previous out-migration of the young, aging-in-place of resident populations, and recent in-migration of older persons, these higher concentrations mean that rural areas, compared to urban places, have a larger percentage of their population in the age category often associated with more needs and fewer resources. This demographic fact may have significant implications for the demand of services for the elderly.

The growth of the elderly population in rural areas since 1950 has been much more rapid than that of the non-elderly population and has contributed significantly to the overall growth of rural places. During the 1960's, nonmetropolitan areas registered a net migration gain of the elderly that not only contributed to the absolute and relative increases in the elderly population, but also preceded and perhaps even was partially responsible for the overall population turnaround recorded in rural areas in the 1970's. Overall, the elderly migrants to nonmetropolitan areas in recent years have been of higher economic and social status than the indigenous elderly population or nonmetropolitan elderly who move to metropolitan places. These gains due to elderly in-migration occurred in all regions of the United States but were particularly strong in certain areas—especially places with mild climates and recreational facilities.

It would appear that the net migration of elderly into rural places in the past two decades has resulted from a combination of factors—a desire for improved climate and recreational opportunities, a return in retirement to a previous residence or vacation place, and perhaps a quest for a better overall quality of life than that available in bigger cities. Researchers are beginning to examine another important aspect of this demographic trend—the impact that elderly migrants have on their new communities of residence. The rather limited amount of work available today on this question indicates that the impact has not been negative, but more research needs to be done.

In addition, it has been noted that the rural elderly differ from their urban counterparts on some basic socio-demographic characteristics. Rural elderly, especially those living on farms, are more likely to be male and to be married. Marital status differences are particularly strong for elderly females: females living on farms are much more likely to be married than urban or even rural nonfarm females. Family status differences are also found based on residence and sex, with the rural elderly, especially females, less likely to live alone.

Finally, a number of issues of great importance concerning demographic trends among the rural elderly that need to be more fully investigated have been identified. Most of these revolve around the net migration gains of elderly persons in rural areas. Clearly, the impact of such movements could be of major consequence to many of the basic institutions in rural areas. The nature and degree of this impact and the response to it will of necessity command more and more attention from demographers and rural gerontologists.

REFERENCES

Aday, R.H., and L.A. Miles. 1982, "Long-Term Impacts of Rural Migration of the Elderly: Implications for Research," *The Gerontologist*, 22, 331–336.

Barsby, S.L., and D.R. Cox. 1975, *Interstate Migration of the Elderly*, D.E., Heath, New York.

Beale, C.L. 1975, *The Revival of Population Growth in Nonmetropolitan America*, U.S. Department of Agriculture, Economic Research Service, ERS–605, Washington, D.C.

———. 1978, "People on the Land," *Rural U.S.A.: Persistence and Change*, T.R. Ford (ed.), Iowa State University Press, Ames, Iowa.

Beale, C.L., and G.V. Fuguitt. 1978, "The New Pattern of Nonmetropolitan Population Change," in *Social Demography*, K.E. Taeuber, L.L. Bumpass, and J.A. Sweet (eds.), Academic Press, New York.

Biggar, J.E. 1980, "Who Moved Among the Elderly, 1965–1970: Comparison of Types of Older Movers," *Research on Aging*, 2, 73–91.

Cebula, R. 1974, "The Quality of Life and Migration of the Elderly," *Review of Regional Studies*, 4, 62–68.

Clifford, W.B., T.B. Heaton, D.T. Lichter, and G.V. Fuguitt. 1983, "Components of Change in the Age Composition of Nonmetropolitan America," *Rural Sociology*, 48, 458–470.

Clifford, W. B., T.B. Heaton, P. Voss, and G.V. Fuguitt. 1985, "The Rural Elderly in Demographic Perspective," in *The Elderly in Rural Society*, R. Coward and G. Lee (eds.), Springer, New York.

Diemling, G.T. and L. Huber. 1981, "The Availability and Participation of Immediate Kin in Caring for the Rural Elderly," paper presented at the annual meeting of the Gerontological Society of America, Toronto, Canada, November.

Ecosometrics. 1981, *Review of Reported Differences Between the Rural and Urban Elderly: Status, Needs, Services, and Service Costs*, final report to the Administration on the Aging (Contract No. 105–80–C–065), Washington, D.C.

Fuguitt, G.V., and S.J. Tordella. 1980, "Elderly Net Migration: The New Trend of Nonmetropolitan Population Change," *Research on Aging*, 2, 191–204.

Golant, S.M. 1975, "Residential Concentrations of the Future Elderly," *The Gerontologist*, 15, 16–23.

———. 1979, "Central City, Suburban, and Nonmetropolitan Area Migration Patterns of the Elderly," in *Location and Environment of the Elderly Population*, S.M. Golant (ed.), V.H. Winston and Sons, Washington, D.C.

Harbert, W., and K. Wilkinson. 1979, "Growing Old in Rural America," *Aging*, January, 36–40.

Heintz, K.M. 1976, *Retirement Communities*, Center for Urban Policy Research, New Brunswick, New Jersey.

Johnson, K.K., and R.L. Purdy. 1980, "Recent Nonmetropolitan Population Change in Fifty Year Perspective," *Demography*, 17, 57–70.

Kim, P.K. 1981, "The Low Income Rural Elderly: Under-Served Victims of Public Inequity," in *Toward Mental Health of the Rural Elderly*, P.K. Kim and C. Wilson (eds.), University Press of America, Washington, D.C.

Koebernick, T.E., and J.A. Beegle. 1978, "Migration of the Elderly to Rural Areas: A Case Study in Michigan," in *Patterns of Migration and Population Change in America's Heartland*, Research Report No. 344, Agriculture Experiment Station, Michigan State University, East Lansing, Michigan.

Krout, J.A. 1983, "Seasonal Migration of the Elderly," *The Gerontologist*, 23, 295–299.

Lee, A.S. 1980, "Aged Migration: Impact on Service Delivery," *Research On Aging*, 2, 243–253.

Lee, G.R., and M.L. Lassey. 1982, "The Elderly," in *Rural Society in the U.S.: Issues for the 1980's*, D.A. Dillman and D.J. Hobbs (eds.), Westview Press, Boulder, Colorado.

Lichter, D.T., G.V. Fuguitt, T.S. Heaton, and W.B. Clifford. 1981, "Components of Change in the Residential Concentration of the Elderly Population: 1950–1975," *Journal Of Gerontology*. 36, 480– 489.

Longino, C.F. 1980, "Residential Relocation of Older People—Metropolitan and Nonmetropolitan," *Research on Aging*, 2, 205–216.

Longino, C.F., and J.C. Biggar. 1981, "The Impact of Retirement and Migration on the South," *The Gerontologist*, 21, 283–290.

McCarthy, K.F., and P.A. Morrison. 1979, *The Changing Demographic and Economic Structure of Nonmetropolitan Areas in the United States*, Rand Corporation, Santa Monica, California.

Monahan, D.J., and V.L. Greene. 1982, "The Impact of Seasonal Population Fluctuations upon Service Delivery," *The Gerontologist*, 22, 160–163.

Roseman, E.E. 1977, *Changing Migration Patterns Within the United States*, Resource Papers for College Geography No. 77–2, Association of American Geographers, Washington, D.C.

Schwarzweller, H. 1979, "Migration and the Changing Rural Scene," *Rural Sociology*, 33, 7–23.

Serow, W.J. 1978, "Return Migration of the Elderly in the U.S.A.: 1955– 1960 and 1965–1970," *Journal Of Gerontology*, 33, 288–295.

Shaw, R.P. 1975, *Migration Theory and Fact*, Regional Science Research Institute, Philadelphia.

Siegel, J.S. 1979, "Prospective Trends in the Size and Structure of the Elderly Population, Impact of Mortality Trends and Some Implications," Current Population Reports, Series P–23, No. 82, United States Bureau of the Census, Washington, D.C.

Sofranko, A.J., J.D. Williams, and F.C. Fliegel. 1981, "Urban Migrants to the Rural Midwest: Some Understandings and Misunderstandings," in *Population Redistribution in the Midwest*, E.E. Roseman et al. (eds.), North Central Regional Center for Rural Development, Iowa State University Press, Ames, Iowa.

Soldo, B. 1980, "America's Elderly in the 1980's," *Population Bulletin*, 35, 15–18.

Taeuber, I.B. 1972, "The Changing Distribution of the Population in the United States in the Twentieth Century," in *Population Distribution and Policy*, vol. 5, S.M. Mazie (ed.), Commission on Population Growth and the American Future, Washington, D.C.

Tucker, C.J. 1976, "Changing Rural Areas in the United States: Recent Evidence," *Demography*, 13, 435–443.

Voss, P.R., and G.V. Fuguitt. 1979, *Turnaround Migration in the Upper Great Lakes Region*, Applied Population Laboratory, Population Series 70–12, Department of Rural Sociology, University of Wisconsin, Madison, Wisconsin.

Ward, R. 1984, *The Aging Experience*, Harper and Row, New York.

Weeks, J. 1984, *Aging: Concepts and Issues*, Wadsworth Publishing, Belmont, California.

Williams, J., and A. Sofranko. 1979, "Motivations for the Inmigration Component of Population Turnaround in Nonmetropolitan Areas," *Demography*, 16, 239–255.

Wiseman, R.F. 1979, "Regional Patterns of Elderly Concentration and Migration," in *Location and Environment of Elderly Population*, S.M. Golant (ed.), V.H. Winston and Sons, Washington, D.C.

Yu, W., and M.D. Van Arsdol, Jr. 1977, "Residential Mobility, Age, and the Life Cycle," *Journal of Gerontology*, 32, 211–221.

Zuiches, J.J. and D.L. Brown. 1978, "The Changing Character of the Nonmetropolitan Population, 1950–1975," in *Rural U.S.A: Persistence and Change*. T.R. Ford (ed.), Iowa State University Press, Ames, Iowa.

3 ECONOMIC STATUS

INTRODUCTION

Perhaps the most commonly used indicator of well-being in America is income and the economic status that accompanies it. Low income is associated with a plethora of needs such as housing, health and health care, and transportation, as well as more subjective factors such as life satisfaction. Problems stemming from lack of income have long been associated with being old. The elderly have been over-represented among the poor as reduced incomes due to retirement and inadequate savings were further eroded by the inflation of the 1960's and 1970's. And while the development of private and public programs during the past 10 to 20 years has resulted in significant economic gains for the elderly (Schulz, 1980), the aged as a group have lower incomes than the non-elderly. In 1980, for example, the median income for families headed by individuals aged 65 and over was $12,881—lower than any other age group. This figure was $27,256 for those 45–54 and $23,531 for those 55–64. Income for individuals was lower but followed the same age-related pattern (U.S. Bureau of the Census, 1981).

As for the adequacy of such income levels, the elderly are often seen as much more likely to have incomes below the official poverty line. Recent data show that the elderly are no longer more likely to be poor than the non-elderly (Ward, 1984). However, a greater percentage of elderly are more likely to be "near poor"—to have an income of less than 125 percent of the poverty line income.

Of course these income figures are for the elderly as a group and are misleading because the elderly are not a homogeneous group. Considerable differences in income exist based on sex, race, employment status, and residence. Females and nonwhites have lower incomes, and rural families have higher incomes than urban families (U.S. Bureau of the Census, 1981). In addition, the impact of nonmoney or in-kind income such as tax relief and goods or services received for free or at reduced cost (Medicare, subsidized housing, food stamps) must be considered in an examination of the elderly's economic well-being. These are important for determining the adequacy of income levels. This chapter examines differences on income, income adequacy, and economic status for the aged based on residence.

RURAL VERSUS URBAN ELDERLY INCOME DIFFERENCES

Numerous studies have noted that the incomes of the rural elderly are substantially less than those of the elderly living in metropolitan places. For example, Ossafsky (1978) notes that the median income of the rural elderly is 20 percent below that of the metropolitan elderly, with 40 percent of the former reporting incomes of less than $5,000. Bylund et al. (1980) report that the 1975 median income for elderly-headed households was 14.2 percent below the national average, while the metropolitan average was 3.9 percent above it ($4,440 vs. $5,375). These rural/urban differences were especially notable for population subgroupings based on sex and race. Data analyzed from the 1970 census by Youmans (1977) indicate that elderly nonfarm residents had incomes slightly lower than elderly farm residents. Data from the 1980 census indicates that the rural income disadvantage still exists.

Why do the rural elderly have lower incomes than their urban counterparts? No comprehensive studies have been carried out that adequately answer this question, but the existing research does suggest several reasons. It has been argued that the lifetime earnings of the rural elderly are lower due to the less adequate wage scale of such places in general (New York State Senate, 1980; Twente, 1970; White House Conference on Aging, 1973). The rural elderly are more likely to have worked in occupations that were not covered by the Social Security Act. Each of these would result in lower Social Security payments to the rural elderly. These payments are by far the largest source of income for the elderly, especially for certain groups such as females and those living alone (Schulz, 1980). One study noted that even though one-third of the Social Security beneficiaries live in rural areas, they receive 10 percent lower benefits than the urban elderly (Kim, 1981). Thompson (1978, 1979) reports that the urban elderly receive a greater proportion of their income from other sources, including pensions, than the rural elderly. Other sources of income for the elderly include interest on savings and dividends from investments. The rural elderly are only one-half as likely to have either of these (Auerbach, 1975).

POVERTY AMONG THE RURAL ELDERLY

As would be expected from the findings just presented, statistics indicate that the rural elderly are more likely to be classified as poor or to have incomes below the government's official poverty level. Just how much more likely depends on the study one refers to. For example, Kim (1981) argues that the rural elderly are twice as likely to be poor as are their urban counterparts. Recent data from the U.S. Census Bureau (1981) support this assertion. In 1980, 12 percent of the metropolitan elderly fell below the poverty line, while 20.5 percent of the nonmetropolitan elderly were poor. More detailed data by community type are available for 1979 and are presented in Table 3.1.

Data in Table 3.1 indicate that regardless of whether one refers to elderly living in families or alone, the percentage of elderly with incomes below the poverty level is almost twice as great in nonmetropolitan areas as in metropolitan areas. Within metropolitan places, those elderly residing in urban areas but outside the central city were least likely to be poor, while those residing in rural places were most likely to be in poverty. Rural

TABLE 3.1

Percentage of Elderly Living In Families or Living Alone with Incomes Below the
Poverty Level for Nonmetropolitan and Metropolitan Areas, 1979

	Living In Families	Living Alone
METROPOLITAN AREAS		
Total	6.2	24.6
Urban		
Total	5.8	23.7
Central cities	7.2	26.8
Not in central cities	4.4	21.9
Rural	9.1	32.4
NONMETROPOLITAN AREAS		
Total	12.7	37.7
Urban	9.2	33.9
Rural	14.8	41.0

Source: 1980 Census of Population, Volume 1, Characteristics of the Population,
Chapter C, General Social and Economic Characteristics, Part I, United
States Summary, Table 109, U.S. Bureau of the Census, December 1983.

elderly living in nonmetropolitan areas were more likely than
any other group to be poor.

The divergence based on residence type in combination with
family status is striking indeed. Only 4.4 percent of metropolitan
non–central-city elderly living in families were poor in 1979, in
contrast with 41.0 percent for elderly individuals living alone in
rural nonmetropolitan areas. Another way to express the rural
elderly income disadvantage is to note that while approximately
36 percent of the nation's elderly lived in nonmetropolitan areas,
44 percent of the nation's poor elderly live in such places (Kim,
1981). Sixty-one percent of these poor rural elderly had 1977
incomes below $2,000, and 81 percent had incomes below $4,000.

Once again, these statistics hide the status of groups within
the overall elderly population. For example, the poverty rate for
blacks aged 60 and over is three times that of whites (11 percent

versus 33 percent), but the rate for rural blacks is 40 percent. And over one-half of the rural blacks aged 72 and over are categorized as poor. This serves to point out several important observations in regard to using income as an indicator of the relative economic status of the rural elderly. First, rural/urban differences may not be as large as differences based on other factors such as race, sex, and whether or not someone lives alone (Ecosometrics, 1981). Second, nonetheless, rural residence compounds the disadvantaged status of various segments of the elderly population, producing what has been called triple jeopardy (New York State Senate, 1980). Finally, one other geographic variation is worthy of mention—elderly living in the South, urban or rural, are more likely to be below the poverty levels than elderly living in other regions of the nation.

INCOME AS AN INDICATOR OF ECONOMIC WELL-BEING

It was suggested at the beginning of this chapter that income in and of itself is not necessarily an accurate or the most appropriate indicator of the economic status of the elderly or the differences between the rural and urban elderly. Unfortunately, most of the comparisons of the rural/urban elderly utilize only income data, so little information is available on the impact of non-income factors. The main criticism of income as a measure of economic well-being is that it excludes factors such as in-kind transfers (the receipt of services at no or reduced cost) and non-income assets such as houses. In addition, cost-of-living differences based on residence should also be considered in such comparisons.

In fact, there is some evidence to suggest that these other factors increase the economic status of the elderly in general and may reduce the rural/urban differences based on income alone. One comprehensive study of the economic welfare of the elderly (Moon, 1977) using 1967 census data found that the nonmetropolitan elderly had mean money incomes 20 percent less than the metropolitan suburban elderly and 13 percent less than the central city elderly. When other economic welfare measures were included, the nonmetropolitan elderly were found to have an economic status 14 percent below the suburban elderly and equal to that of the central city elderly. This decrease in disparity presumably was caused by the fact that the nonmetropolitan elderly had greater assets (for example, they are considerably more likely to own their own home). Other research (Ecosometrics, 1981) on rural/urban differences found a rural sample of elderly more likely to receive Supplemental Security Income (SSI) payments, food stamps, and Medicaid, although they were less likely to get income from rental interest, investments, and retirement pensions. Yet at least one author (Kim, 1981) argues that the SSI payment figures set by the Social Security Administration actually operate to the disadvantage of the rural elderly.

Further, it can be argued that the lower cost of living in rural areas somewhat offsets the lower money income levels of the rural elderly and contributes to closing the gap between the economic status of the urban and rural elderly. In general, the guidelines established by the government set the poverty line 15 percent higher for farm families (Kim, 1981). That is, it is assumed that farm families need less money to live on. Lipman (1978) notes that this reflects the capability of farm families to meet some of their own food needs. However, only 16 percent of the rural elderly households actually live on farms (Ecosometrics, 1981).

Do the rural elderly spend less for the basic necessities? Data from the U.S. Bureau of Labor Standards (1981) show that the elderly living in nonmetropolitan urban areas (2,500–50,000) have budgets that are 85 percent of those of the metropolitan elderly with comparable living standards. They spend less in each budget category but proportionately less only on housing. The interpretation of these data is open to question. Some (Kim, 1981) argue that the actual cost of living may be higher for the rural elderly due to their greater isolation from a variety of goods and services.

The preceding discussion has raised several important issues concerning the economic status of the rural elderly. While the literature consistently states that the rural elderly are worse off economically than the urban elderly, a closer examination of this issue reveals that such a conclusion may not be entirely justified. While a comparison of statistics on money income supports a "rural disadvantagement" thesis, the inclusion of in-kind payments and assets may considerably reduce, perhaps even eliminate, the urban edge. Certainly it would appear that income data alone are not sufficient to provide an adequate examination of rural/urban differences of economic well-being or to prove that the rural elderly are worse off.

PERCEPTION OF INCOME ADEQUACY

Findings from research on the elderly's perception of their well-being and needs are also relevant to the discussion of the elderly's economic status. Regardless of income differences, some research suggests that the rural elderly are equally satisfied with their income level. In fact, significant rural/urban differences on the elderly's assessment of their financial situation do not appear to exist. Coward and Kerckhoff (1978) report that 90 percent of a rural elderly sample see income as adequate and only one-fourth indicate any serious financial problems. And Youmans (1963) reports that the rural elderly in Kentucky were slightly less likely to report finances as a serious problem than the urban elderly.

Research conducted by the author (Krout and Larson, 1980) in a nonmetropolitan county found that one-quarter of the over 5,000 elderly respondents said their incomes met their needs very well, 50 percent said fairly well and only 15 percent said not very well. Very small differences were found for elderly who lived in the open country, villages, or small cities. Kivett and Scott (1979), in a study of a sample of North Carolina rural elderly, report that one-quarter of the respondents felt their income was not adequate to meet their needs but that the majority (58 percent) said it was if they were careful. Similar findings are noted in several other North Carolina studies (Kivett, 1976; Kivett and Scott, 1979). Scott and Learner (1977) also investigated the correlates of perceived income adequacy and found that those elderly who were white, older, better educated, or had higher levels of morale were more likely to see their incomes as adequate. Yet Auerbach (1976) found that the rural elderly were twice as likely to state a primary need for money.

The author has suggested elsewhere (Krout and Larson, 1980)

that the self-assessed needs statements of the rural elderly might be influenced by earlier life experiences in the more rural environments of the early 1900's, when the material standard of living was hardly comparable with that of present-day urban society. Thus, their idea of what constitutes adequate income, medical care, transportation, or housing may differ significantly from that of younger people or present-day government standards.

Any statement of needs or problems is, of course, relative to the individual's past experiences, current life circumstances, and the circumstances of others around him or her. It is possible that the city elderly report more needs because they have higher expectations brought about by a greater exposure to affluence and services. Their rural and village counterparts may have a different level of expectations and not view low income or difficulties in access to transportation or medical care as a problem even if the difficulties are there. Research on the elderly, especially in rural areas, shows that they are likely to have spent a large part of the last 20 years living in the same area and thus have had ample time to develop expectations relative to a particular community setting.

This line of thinking boils down to a "relative deprivation" explanation of differences found in the research on self-assessed needs. That is, the elderly's assessments of needs and problems are relative to the expectations they have internalized throughout their life experiences, the present environmental setting in which they live, and their self-concept as an elderly person in relation to the predominant social definition of what an elderly person is and does (Krout and Larson, 1980).

The same may be true of differences based on age. Younger persons may have a different level of expectations because they have spent a greater proportion of their life in a more affluent America. And they may have higher expectations simply because they are younger and feel that they should be participating more actively in the world around them—something that would require better health, more money, and access to transportation (Krout and Larson, 1980).

Or one might also argue along the lines of Marx's concept of "false consciousness." That is, the elderly don't recognize how badly off they really are because their expectations of what is an acceptable living standard are a product of a social and economic structure that defines the elderly as a nonproductive class and thus less deserving of rewards. And members of rural populations, defined as increasingly superfluous in an era of agribusiness, mechanized farming, and big cities, would expect even less (Krout and Larson, 1980).

RESEARCH NEEDS

It is clear that more research is needed to determine the nature and degree of economic status differences of the rural versus urban elderly. Income data alone are insufficient to answer the question of how well off or disadvantaged the rural elderly are. The problem appears to be one of an absence of appropriate data and the tendency of researchers to consider only part of the picture. The central questions would seem to be, Do lower incomes mean significantly different standards of living, and do these lower incomes effect basic needs such as health, recreation, and transportation? That is, what are the consequences of these income differences for the rural elderly, and how can they be most effectively dealt with? Are there factors in rural environments that counteract the potential effects of lower incomes (e.g., lower cost of living, informal supports, supplemental income sources, nonmonetary sources of subsistence)? Do the rural elderly compensate by different expenditure patterns? If so, what are they?

In addition, the heterogeneity of the rural elderly population has been noted as a key underlying factor that must be addressed. What of the variation in the income of the elderly living in different types of rural places and in different areas of the country? The interaction of residence with other determinants of economic status such as sex, race, and occupation needs to be systematically studied. For example, most income studies have focused almost exclusively on older males and ignored females. The dynamic aspects of the rural elderly's economic status also must be given more attention. Key research questions here include how contractions or expansions of rural economies affect the status of the elderly both directly (as workers) and indirectly and how changes in the nature of the rural economy will change the economic status of future elderly cohorts.

Finally, more attention needs to be given to the finding that while having lower incomes, the rural elderly are just as satisfied with their finances as, or more satisfied than, the urban elderly. Does this simply mean that the rural elderly pay less for more or have found ways to provide for needs through non-income means? Or does it mean the rural elderly are content to make do with less and thus do not translate lower incomes into expressions of need? In any event, the causes and consequences of rural versus urban elderly income needs statements must be researched more systematically. The implications for policy-related research on the rural elderly must also be more carefully thought out.

SUMMARY

This chapter has examined the economic status of the rural elderly. Data from both regional studies and the national census indicate that the rural elderly have lower dollar incomes than the urban elderly. This generalization holds true regardless of the rural/urban designation used or the unit for which income data are shown (e.g., family or individual). In fact, it is clear that the income of the elderly is indirectly related to community type. Even within urbanized areas, significantly lower incomes are reported for smaller communities.

Unfortunately, little research has been conducted that would allow a determination as to why this is the case or the degree to which this income disadvantage translates into real quality-of-life differences. In general, lower rural incomes are seen as a reflection of the lower wage scales of rural areas that lead to smaller Social Security and pension payments. The rural elderly are also more likely to have been employed in occupations not covered by Social Security and not to have other sources of income.

Not surprisingly, the rural elderly are also more likely to have incomes below the poverty line. But existing studies have not resolved the question as to whether or not non-income factors such as noncash assets and lower cost of living affect lower rural incomes enough to reduce the poverty level among the elderly. Regardless of the actual income and poverty levels, research indicates that the rural elderly are no more likely to report income dissatisfaction or inadequacy than the urban elderly. It is obvious that much more systematic research needs to be carried out on income, poverty, and adequacy of income differences between the rural and urban elderly. The data necessary to determine the meaning and impact of these differences simply are not available. It is difficult to imagine the development of appropriate, effective, and equitable income support programs for the rural elderly without such information. A considerable task, then, confronts rural gerontologists as basic questions regarding the economic status of the rural elderly remain unanswered.

REFERENCES

Auerbach, A.J. 1976, "The Elderly in Rural Areas: Differences in Urban Areas and Implications for Practice," in *Social Work in Rural Communities*, L. Ginsberg (ed.), Council on Social Work Education, New York.

Bylund, R., N.L. LeRay, and C.O. Crawford. 1980, *Older American Households and Their Housing, 1975: A Metro-Nonmetro Comparison*, Department of Agriculture Economics and Rural Sociology, Pennsylvania State University, University Park, Pennsylvania.

Coward, R.T., and R.K. Kerckhoff. 1978, *The Rural Elderly: Program Guidelines*, Iowa State University, Ames, Iowa.

Ecosometrics. 1981, *Review of Reported Differences Between the Rural and Urban Elderly: Status, Needs, Services, and Service Costs*, final report to the Administration on the Aging (Contract No. 105–80–C–065), Washington, D.C.

Kim, P.K. 1981, "The Low Income Elderly: Under-Served Victims of Public Inequity," in *Toward Mental Health of the Rural Elderly*, P.K. Kim and C. Wilson (eds.), University Press of America, Washington, D.C.

Kivett, V. 1976, *The Aged in North Carolina: Physical, Social, and Environmental Characteristics and Sources of Assistance*, Technical Bulletin No. 237, Agricultural Research Service, North Carolina State University at Raleigh, Raleigh, North Carolina.

Kivett, V., and J. Scott. 1979, *The Rural By-Passed Elderly: Perspectives on Status and Needs*, Technical Bulletin No. 260, Agricultural Research Service, North Carolina State University at Raleigh, Raleigh, North Carolina.

Krout, J.A., and D. Larson. 1980, "Self-Assessed Needs of the Rural Elderly," paper presented at the annual meeting of the Rural Sociological Society, Ithaca, New York, August.

Lipman, A. 1978, "Needs Inconsistencies of the Rural Aged," in *Proceedings of the Workshop on Rural Gerontology, Research in the Northeast*, May 24–27, 1977, Cornell University, Ithaca, New York.

Moon, M. 1977, *The Measurement of Economic Welfare: Its Application to the Aged Poor*, Academic Press, New York.

New York State Senate. 1980, *Old Age and Ruralism: A Case of Double Jeopardy, Report on the Rural Elderly*, New York State Senate, Albany, New York.

Ossafsky, J. 1978, "Aging in Rural Mid-America: Are We up to the Challenge?" in *The Aging in Rural Mid-America: A Symposium on Values for an Evolving Quality of Life*, L. Forester (ed.), Bethany College, Lindberg, Kansas.

Schulz, J.H. 1980, *The Economics of Aging*, Wadsworth, Belmont, California.

Thompson, G.B. 1978, "Pension Coverage and Benefits, 1972: Findings from the Retirement History Study," *Social Security Bulletin*, 41, 3–17.

———. 1979, "Black-White Differences in Private Pensions: Findings from the Retirement History Study," *Social Security Bulletin*, 42, 15–22.

Twente, E. 1970, *Never Too Old*, Jossey-Bass, San Francisco.

U.S. Bureau of the Census. 1981, *Money Income and Poverty Status of Families and Persons in the United States: 1980*, Current Population Reports, Consumer Income, Series P–60, No. 127, U.S. Government Printing Office, Washington, D.C.

U.S. Bureau of Labor Statistics. 1980, *Handbook of Labor Statistics*, Bulletin No. 2070, U.S. Government Printing Office, Washington, D.C.

Ward, R. 1984, *The Aging Experience*, Harper and Row, New York.

White House Conference on Aging. 1973, *Toward a National Policy on Aging: Proceedings of the 1971 White House Conference on Aging*, U.S. Government Printing Office, Washington, D.C.

Youmans, E.G. 1963, *Aging Patterns in a Rural and Urban Area of Kentucky*, Bulletin No. 682, Agriculture Experiment Station, University of Kentucky, Lexington, Kentucky.

———. 1977, "The Rural Aged," *The Annals of the American Academy of Political Science*, 429, 81–90.

4   WORK, RETIREMENT, AND LEISURE

INTRODUCTION

Not too long ago, few Americans had the opportunity to retire. Shorter life expectancy, combined with labor-intensive technologies and an almost oppressive work ethic, resulted in high rates of employment for the elderly. In 1900, nearly two-thirds of the men in this country aged 65 and over worked or were seeking work, while in 1980, employment rates were 20 percent for elderly males and 8 percent for elderly females (White House Conference on the Aging, 1981). Changes in retirement policies (pensions, Social Security), educational upgrading of occupations, the decline of agriculture and self-employment, and a greater acceptance of retirement as a legitimate way of life were no doubt largely responsible for this decline in labor force participation among the elderly (Foner and Schwab, 1981). Moreover, about one-half of the employed elderly work only part-time, and elderly workers are more likely than the non–self-employed elderly to work in agriculture and the service sector and much less likely to be in the blue collar sector. As a result, and as was noted in the previous chapter, elderly workers have significantly lower incomes than non-elderly workers (White House Conference on the Aging, 1981).

Lower rates of employment, coupled with the increasing tendency for people to retire early (two-thirds retire before age 65) and greater life expectancy, have resulted in a lengthening of the number of years an average person spends in retirement. These trends have focused increased attention on questions of adequacy of retirement incomes, adjustment to and satisfaction with retirement, the types of leisure activities the elderly pursue in retirement, and the adequacy and appropriateness of retirement and leisure-related policies and programs. This chapter examines rural/urban differences in the employment rates of the elderly and work satisfaction. In addition, residential differences in retirement and leisure patterns and in retirement satisfaction are studied. Finally, the availability and provision of leisure and recreation services to the rural elderly are also reviewed. The chapter concludes with a discussion of future research needs and a chapter summary.

EMPLOYMENT STATUS

What of rural/urban differences in the employment status of the elderly? On the one hand, it can be argued that the rural elderly find it more difficult to continue working because rural areas generally do not have a large or complex enough economic base to provide jobs for the elderly (New York State Senate, 1980). In addition, federal employment programs have been criticized for being more widespread in cities and spending more dollars in total and on a per capita basis in urban as opposed to rural areas (Kim, 1981; New York State Senate, 1980). On the other hand, it has been argued that the nature of agriculture and other rural occupations allows for a more gradual disengagement from work and a postponement of full retirement to later in life (Bauder and Doerflinger, 1967). The "agricultural ladder" theory, conceptualized by Harris (1950), states that the ideal career pattern for a farmer involves steps characterized by an increasingly greater replacement of the labor role by management functions. Retirement is not an abrupt event, but includes some physical labor (if health permits) and a retention of a landowner or landlord role.

The data from existing research do not provide particularly strong support for either of these arguments. Many studies of employment and retirement among the rural elderly do not allow for comparisons with urban samples, making conclusions regarding the nature and degree of rural/urban differences difficult. In addition, there appears to be a fair amount of variation in the rates of employment for the rural aged reported by different researchers. For example, Kivett and Scott (1979) report that only 6.5 percent of the elderly in a rural North Carolina county were employed either full- or part-time, considerably less than the 20 percent reported for another sample of North Carolina rural elderly (Kivett, 1976). Larson and Youmans (1978) report that 16 percent of the households in a rural Kentucky sample had elderly members still active in the labor force. Kivett (1976) found that residence was one of several variables (sex, age, social status, and prior occupational status) significantly related to work status.

Data are also not available on the types of jobs the rural elderly hold and how they differ from the urban elderly in this regard. It would appear fairly obvious that the rural elderly are more likely be involved with agriculture since they are more likely to have been so before they reached age 65. In fact, Coffin and LeRay (1979) note that 1974 Census of Agriculture data indicate 18.5 percent of U.S. farm operators were 65 and over with one-half of these located in the South, a region that also had the largest percentage of farms operated by the elderly. Kivett (1976) reports that one-half of the fully employed rural elderly in her study reported working in manual or semi-skilled jobs.

WORK SATISFACTION

As for work satisfaction, it would appear that those rural elderly who work are quite satisfied with their employment. Kivett (1976) reports that 93 percent of the fully employed elderly from a rural and urban North Carolina sample were "very happy" with their work and 73 percent indicated they would continue to work in the next five years. Three-quarters of those elderly working part-time had no plans to retire. These findings are not surprising given the fact that research in general indicates that older workers express greater job satisfaction than younger workers (Mortimer and Lorence, 1979; Wright and Hamilton, 1978). Unfortunately, very little information is available on rural/

urban differences in work satisfaction among the employed elderly.

It can be stated with some confidence, then, that the relatively small number of elderly (rural or urban) who work are to a large extent satisfied with their employment status. But does this mean that those who work are doing so by preference and that those elderly who do not (those retired) have retired by choice? A discussion of these issues is made difficult because of semantic distinctions involving the use of words such as "choice." For example, much attention has been focused on "forced" or "mandatory" retirement—usually a reference to a business's policy of requiring people to stop working at age 65. The 1978 amendment to the Age Discrimination Employment Act set the youngest age for forced retirement in most jobs at 70 (Weeks, 1984). But people can be "forced" to retire by poor health or a plant shutdown, or "forced" to continue working because of economic need.

RETIREMENT

It would appear that the majority of those people who retire before age 65 do so voluntarily or at least willingly. First, recall the significant increase over the past few decades in early retirement. Second, a number of studies show that only a relatively small minority of retirees indicate they would prefer to be working. For example, Streib and Schneider (1971) report that one-third of those workers who retired as a result of company policy were reluctant to do so. Many others were willing to retire. A national survey by the National Council on the Aging (1975) found that while nearly one-third of retirees said they would like to work, only 11 percent would actually consider taking a job. And a 1978 Harris Poll (Harris, 1978) found that 71 percent of the sample preferred to retire early and only 15 percent indicated they preferred to retire at age 65. That would leave 14 percent indicating a preference to retire after age 65.

An examination of the reasons given by individuals for retirement also sheds some light on these issues. Weeks (1984) categorizes reasons for retirement into five areas: poor health, compulsory retirement, being laid off or having a job discontinued, being dissatisfied with a job, and preferring to enjoy free time and take care of family obligations. Keep in mind that there is a close association between the reasons for retirement and the timing or age of retirement. For example, the Social Security Administration (1976) found that more than half of the males retiring prior to age 65 but only one-quarter of those retiring at 65 cited poor health as the most important reason for their retirement. For women, the leading causes are family reasons and poor health (Rosenfeld and Brown, 1979). It would appear that only a small percentage of the elderly retire because of unemployment or job dissatisfaction (Weeks, 1984) and that retiring because one wants to is fairly prevalent. Several studies have indicated that when excluding those who retire for health reasons, 40 percent of those who retire do so because they want to (Motley, 1978).

The available research on the rural elderly is consistent with the general literature on this subject. For example, Kivett (1976) reports that 47 percent of the retired elderly in a North Carolina nonmetropolitan county reported retiring for health reasons but of their own accord, while 17 percent indicated a preference for leisure, 13 percent cited compulsory retirement, and 14 percent noted a combination of reasons. In another study of the rural North Carolina elderly, Kivett and Scott (1979) reported that one-quarter of those elderly who were retired indicated that compulsory retirement was the main reason for their leaving the work force.

RETIREMENT SATISFACTION

The gerontological literature also indicates that the large majority of the elderly view their retirement positively—especially those with higher levels of income, education, and occupation (Ward, 1984). Positive views are found to be held by up to 80 percent of elderly retirees (Parnes, 1981). Again, there is little evidence to suggest that the rural elderly are any different in this regard. Kivett and Scott (1979) report that one-half of the elderly retirees from a rural North Carolina county liked retirement very much, while 28 percent had no strong feeling and only 18 percent were dissatisfied. Of those dissatisfied with retirement, 16 percent wanted to work or be more active or felt a loss of status, 24 percent disliked the extra free time, 15 percent noted poor health, and almost one-half noted a combination of reasons. Those elderly who were female, had a positive self-assessment of health, and were content with the frequency of contact with family and friends were more likely to be very satisfied.

Gowdy et al. (1982) argue that one important indicator of retirement satisfaction is job deprivation—a feeling of missing work. They note that several studies indicate a low percentage of such a feeling among the elderly in general (Glamser, 1981; Kimmel et al., 1978) but that very little research is available on this topic for the rural elderly—especially farmers. Their study of Iowa farmers indicates that 9 percent of retired farmers could be classified as having "high" job deprivation, 20 percent as medium, and 71 percent as low. Part-time workers were even more likely to score low levels of job deprivation (82 percent). Job deprivation was found to be related to three types of factors: work, retirement adjustment, and socio-economic. Those retired elderly farmers who felt their health had interfered with their work before retiring or saw themselves as worse off than others their own age reported higher levels of job deprivation, as did those who reported greater difficulty in adjusting to retirement. In addition, it was found that retired farmers reported less actual job deprivation than anticipated by full-time working farmers.

LEISURE

Leisure, or activities engaged in voluntarily during one's free time for intrinsic satisfaction, encompasses a wide range of activities. Such activities are seen as particularly important in the lives of the elderly whose retirement status leaves them with much time to engage in leisure or recreational pursuits. In addition, gerontologists have devoted a considerable amount of research on the elderly's leisure activities because of their impact on mental and physical health and personal growth and development (Ward, 1984).

While the aged in general are more likely to spend time in solitary or sedentary activities and less likely to engage in active and enriching behavior (Kaplan, 1979; Lawton, 1978; Moss and Lawton, 1982), society by and large tends to overexaggerate their passivity. In fact, the majority of the elderly in the United States do pursue a wide variety of leisure/recreation pursuits. Harris (1978) reports that a national sample of elderly shows that they spend a lot of their time at the following: 47 percent socializing with friends, 39 percent gardening or raising plants, 36 percent reading or watching television, and 25 percent walking and other hobbies. There is no specific type of retirement activity but rather a wide range of undertakings.

The literature does indicate that differences in both attitudes toward leisure and leisure behavior do exist based on variables such as sex and socio-economic status (Ward, 1984). For example, lower income elderly are more likely to watch television, spend time with family members, hunt and fish, and engage in hobbies than the higher income elderly, who are more inclined to travel, partake in cultural activities, or join clubs (Ward, 1984). These observed differences among the general elderly population suggest that considerable variation may exist among the rural elderly as well.

In the rest of this chapter, a number of aspects of leisure/recreation among the rural elderly will be examined, including recreational interests and behaviors, characteristics of rural areas and the rural elderly that affect the provision of leisure/recreation activities, and various ways in which the leisure/recreational needs of the rural elderly can be met. It should be noted that the available research consists largely of studies of single communities and generalizations either about the rural elderly as a whole or about rural/urban comparisons based on this literature are risky at best. This point is of particular significance given the recognized diversity of rural environments.

It would appear that the rural elderly, like other elderly, participate in a wide variety of leisure activities. Youmans and Larson (1977) report that 29 percent of the males and 45 percent of the females of a rural Kentucky sample expressed a need for recreational activities such as games, crafts, and visiting. Kivett and Scott (1979) report that 85 percent of a sample of North Carolina elderly rated watching television as their favorite leisure activity. Other studies have shown differences based on sex and age. For example, Pihlblad et al. (1976) found greater rates of participation in social and recreational organizations for females as opposed to males for a sample of 1,700 rural elderly Missourians. Hoar (1961), in a study of Mississippi elderly, found that women in their 60's and 70's identified loafing, reading, and gardening as their most common leisure activities, while the most common pursuits for men in their 60's were gardening, watching television, and fishing or hunting. Leisure activities for older males were more sedentary. Men in their 70's noted pursuits such as watching television, resting, and reading.

Several studies attest to the importance of the church in the leisure activities of the rural elderly. Hughston et al. (1979) report that 70 percent of a sample of Virginia elderly participate in church activities, followed by 45 percent in cooking and 43 percent in gardening. And Pihlblad et al. (1976) note that a rural Missouri sample of elderly reported low participation in formal social activities except for church membership.

It would seem logical to expect some leisure activity differences between the rural and urban elderly based on some of the differences already noted for these two groups. For example, the rural elderly are more likely to be male and married (especially the farm elderly), to have lower incomes, and to value independence. In addition, rural areas by definition have lower densities of population, are more likely to have agriculture-related industries, have little public transportation, and have fewer organizational resources to provide formalized recreation services. And the rural elderly may have had different socialization and historical experiences.

Thus, one might hypothesize that the rural elderly would be more likely to engage in leisure pursuits such as gardening, fishing, and hunting simply because of the greater availability and accessibility of land and undeveloped countryside, previous experience in agriculture, and the "outdoors" tradition of rural America. Lack of public transportation and less availability of services might result in a lower rate of usage of formal leisure activities such as those available at senior centers. Solitary leisure pursuits or simple visiting of friends could also be expected to be more frequent among the rural elderly.

Unfortunately, very few studies have been carried out that

allow rural/urban comparisons. Residence has usually not been included as a variable in leisure/recreation studies. It would appear that church-related activities are of particular importance to the rural elderly (Hughston et al., 1979; Pihlblad et al., 1967). Several studies have reported small differences between rural and urban samples. Youmans (1962), in a comparison of rural and urban elderly living in Kentucky, found the urban elderly more likely to participate in formal activities and the rural elderly more likely to participate in activities involving just friends. Auerbach (1976) compared the leisure activities of a sample of elderly living in Chicago to one living in rural Illinois and found that television was the most popular activity of each group. The urban sample was more likely to read newspapers, books, and periodicals, and less likely to attend church and social clubs. Nonetheless, a number of studies of a wide range of recreation/leisure programs in rural areas all over the country have reported such programs have positive impacts on the elderly's health and social and psychological well-being (Leitner et al., 1980). These include programs such as exercise and physical activity, nutrition, and social interaction (games, trips, and group discussions).

LEISURE/RECREATION SERVICES

Very little comparative data is available on rural/urban differences in the number, nature, and quality of leisure/recreational activities and services. The literature would seem to suggest that rural areas, with their smaller tax bases and lower densities of population, have fewer such activities. The author (Krout, 1983) has conducted a study that provides some empirical data on this issue. In a 1983 survey of 755 senior centers in 31 states, the author found the mean number of recreation services offered by senior centers directly related to the size of the community in which the center was located. While centers in metropolitan central cities reported a mean of 3.65 recreational services, non-metropolitan urban (2,500 and up) centers reported a mean of 3.41 and nonmetropolitan rural reported a mean of 2.97. In addition, the availability of such activities (frequency of offering) was also lower in nonmetropolitan places.

It would appear that the provision of leisure recreation programs and activities to the rural elderly must overcome a number of obstacles that are different in kind or degree from those found in more urbanized areas. First, the ecology of rural areas must be considered. Rural areas, with their smaller populations and lower population densities (greater distances between people and places), are faced with particularly difficult transportation problems that make the reliance on centralized leisure/recreation programs inappropriate. Kivett (1979) identifies lack of transportation as a major obstacle to social activity intervention programs for the rural elderly. And Larson and Youmans (1978) report that one-half of their sample of rural elderly indicated that they would need transportation assistance to attend a senior center if it were available. The geographic dispersion of the rural elderly not only increases the transportation costs associated with providing leisure programs to the elderly, it also makes it more difficult to offer a wide range of activities.

Second, the economic and organizational resources of many rural communities may not be adequate to support significant leisure programs. Rural service providers may not have adequate levels of training (DeJong and Bishop, 1980), nor do small communities always have the resources to obtain outside funding or to take advantage of federal funds, with their cumbersome rules and regulations (Steinhauer, 1980).

Third, the attitudes and characteristics of the rural elderly themselves also impact on leisure activity programming and provision. It has been noted that some studies indicate a tendency for the rural elderly to apparently understate needs (Auerbach, 1976), possibly because of their desire to be and to appear to be self-reliant and nondependent (Coward, 1979). In fact, one study (Berry and Stinson, 1977) found that while only 12.4 percent of rural service providers stated that the rural elderly had enough recreational services, 78.4 percent of an elderly sample said the same. This points to a potentially significant issue—the gap between service provider's and the target population's perception of need.

In addition, the large diversity between rural areas and rural elderly populations in different areas also affects the planning and provision of such services. Several studies (Bastida, 1980; Vinson and Gallagher, 1980) have shown that differences in the leisure interests of the rural elderly exist on racial and ethnic lines. Moreover, leisure/recreational needs and interests are also related to the sex, educational, and health status of the rural elderly (Hooyman and Scott, 1979). Thus, leisure/recreational programs should not be introduced into rural areas without benefit of a thorough needs assessment (Leitner et al, 1980).

All of these points suggest that generalizations on the leisure/recreation needs and interests of the rural elderly are not easily formulated or documented and sensitivity to a wide range of factors is necessary if appropriate and effective leisure programming is to result. It would appear that traditional centralized urban service delivery models are inappropriate. Special attention must be given to transportation coordination (Ambrosius, 1979), and an emphasis should be placed on creative provision strategies such as mobile recreational service vehicles or roving activity specialists (Leitner et al., 1980).

The rural elderly themselves should be included as much as possible in the planning, implementing, and evaluation of leisure/recreation programs and institutions with particular significance to the rural elderly, such as the church, should also be involved (Karcher and Karcher, 1980). In addition, the realities of rural areas demand a greater cooperation of agencies and sharing of resources (Coward, 1979) and a greater communication between public and private leisure/recreational services (Vinson and Gallagher, 1980).

RESEARCH NEEDS

This chapter has identified a number of questions concerning work, retirement, and leisure patterns of the rural elderly that will require considerably more attention from researchers and practitioners if an adequate knowledge base on these important topics is to be forthcoming. In terms of work, there is a need for more census data on the amount and nature of employment patterns of the rural versus urban elderly. To the degree that rural elderly males work to later ages, the reasons for this must be more clearly identified. And what of retirement patterns? Very little comparative data is available on how the causes and consequences of retirement for rural and urban elderly differ.

Are there differences based on residence in the elderly's desire to work and ability to find jobs that meet their interests? And what of reasons for and adjustment to retirement? The available research, while limited, does not point to significant differences in retirement satisfaction.

Turning to leisure/recreation, while some research has been carried out on rural/urban differences in leisure activities, many questions have not been adequately addressed. For example, it is not clear if the rural elderly have a greater need or desire for formal leisure activities or how consistently leisure interests differ from their urban counterparts. Indeed, the variation just among rural areas and elderly populations has been woefully neglected. There is considerable need to examine how residence interacts with factors such as race, sex, and health status in forming leisure interests and patterns. It has been suggested that a number of characteristics of rural places and people create unique problems for leisure service provision. Solutions to these and other issues have not been systematically examined.

SUMMARY

Employment rates for the elderly have declined steadily in the last several decades, producing an increased interest among gerontologists in the employment, retirement, and leisure patterns of the elderly. This chapter has examined a number of issues related to these topics in regard to the rural elderly, including employment status and satisfaction, reasons for and satisfaction with retirement, leisure activities, and the provision of leisure/recreation services. Overall, there is relatively little comparative research available on rural/urban differences on these topics or even work that documents the nature and scope of variation within rural areas. The existing literature does not adequately document how residence per se affects employment, retirement, and leisure patterns.

Studies suggest that the rural elderly are at least as likely as, and perhaps more likely than, the urban elderly to work and, not surprisingly, are more likely to be involved in agriculture. The rural elderly appear to evidence levels of work and retirement satisfaction and reasons for retirement similar to those of the general elderly population. They participate in a wide variety of leisure activities and do have some leisure/recreation patterns that seem to be associated with rural environments and culture. It would appear that church-related and informal activities are of particular importance to the rural elderly.

The literature indicates that formal leisure programs are less available to the rural elderly and that both their availability and accessibility are significantly affected by the ecological, economic, cultural, and organizational characteristics of rural areas. That is, rural areas in general have fewer economic and organizational resources yet are faced with obstacles to service provision such as transportation problems due to low population density and a resistance to or non-acceptance of formal services due to the elderly's attitudes and values. These obstacles necessitate the development of leisure/recreation service programs and delivery strategies that build on the strengths of rural areas and utilize existing resources in innovative and cost-effective ways.

Clearly, a knowledge gap exists concerning the work, retirement, and leisure patterns of the rural elderly. Models of rural/ urban differences in these areas are rare, and the existing empirical research consists largely of community case studies with few systematic rural/urban comparisons or examinations of the variation that exists within rural/nonmetropolitan places. Data from such studies are needed if policies and programs responsive to rural realities are to be forthcoming.

REFERENCES

Ambrosius, G.R. 1979, *A Report on National Rural Strategy Conference to Improve Service Delivery to Rural Elderly*, Iowa Lakes Area Agency on Aging, Spencer, Iowa.

Auerbach, A. 1976, "The Elderly in Rural Areas: Differences in Urban Areas and Implications for Practice," in *Social Work in Rural Communities: A Book of Readings*, L.H. Ginsberg (ed.), Council on Social Work Education, New York.

Bastida, E. 1980, "The Rural Minority Elderly: In Greater Isolation and Need," *The Gerontologist*, 20, 62.

Bauder, W., and J. Doerflinger. 1967, "Work Roles Among the Rural

Aged," in *Older Rural Americans*, E.G. Youmans (ed.), University of Kentucky Press, Lexington, Kentucky.

Berry, C.G., and F.S. Stinson. 1977, *Service Consumption Patterns and Service Priorities of the Elderly*, Contract No. HEW–105–74–3104, Administration on Aging, Washington, D.C.

Coffin, J., and N. LeRay. 1979, *Older Farm Operators and Their Farms*, Economic Development Division, Economics, Statistics, and Cooperative Services, U.S. Department of Agriculture, Washington, D.C.

Coward, R.T. 1979, "Planning Community Services for the Rural Elderly: Implications from Research," *The Gerontologist*, 19, 275–282.

DeJong, F.J., and C.J. Bishop. 1980, "The View from the Country," *The Gerontologist*, 20, 91.

Foner, A., and K. Schwab. 1981, *Aging and Retirement*, Brooks/Cole Publishing Company, Monterey, California.

Glamser, F.D. 1981, "Predictors of Retirement Attitudes," *Aging and Work*. 4, 23–29.

Gowdy, W., S. Burke, E. Powers, and P. Keith. 1982, "Job Deprivation Among Older Farmers," paper presented at the annual meeting of the Rural Sociological Society, San Francisco, September.

Harris, C.S. 1978, *Fact Book on Aging: A Profile of America's Older Population*, National Council on the Aging, Washington, D.C.

Harris, M. 1950, "A New Agricultural Ladder," *Land Economics*, 26, 258–267.

Hoar, J. 1961, "A Study of Free-Time Activities of 200 Aged Persons," *Sociology and Social Research*, 45, 157–163.

Hooyman, N., and N. Scott. 1979, "A Mutual Help Model for Rural Older Women," *The Gerontologist*, 19, 91.

Hughston, G., L. Axelson, and J.F. Keller. 1979, "Leisure Time Preferences of the Elderly: Family Ties, Responsibilities, and Reflections," paper presented at the Recreation and Park Association Annual Congress, New Orleans.

Kaplan, M. 1979, *Leisure: Lifestyle And Lifespan*. W.E. Saunders, Philadelphia.

Karcher, C.J., and B.C. Karcher. 1980, "Higher Education and Religion: Potential Partners in Services to the Rural Elderly," *Educational Gerontology: An International Journal*, 5, 409–421.

Kim, P.K. 1981, "The Low Income Rural Elderly: Under-Served Victims of Public Inequity," in *Toward Mental Health of the Rural Elderly*, P. Kim and C. Wilson (eds.), University Press of America, Washington, D.C.

Kimmel, D.C., F.K. Price, and J.W. Walker. 1978, "Retirement Choice and Retirement Satisfaction," *Journal Of Gerontology*, 33, 575–585.

Kivett, V. 1976, *The Aged in North Carolina: Physical, Social and Environmental Characteristics and Sources of Assistance*, Technical Bulletin No. 237, Agricultural Research Service, North Carolina State University at Raleigh, Raleigh, North Carolina.

Kivett, V., and J. Scott. 1979, *The Rural By-Passed Elderly: Perspectives on Status and Needs*, Technical Bulletin No. 260, Agricultural Research Service, North Carolina State University at Raleigh, Raleigh, North Carolina.

Krout, J.A. 1983, *The Organization, Operation, and Programming of Senior Centers: A National Survey*, Final Report to the Andrus Foundation, American Association of Retired Persons, Fredonia, New York.

Larson, D.K., and E.G. Youmans. 1978, *Problems of Rural Elderly Households in Powell County, Kentucky*, Economic Development Division, Economics, Statistics, and Cooperative Service, U.S. Department of Agriculture, Washington, D.C.

Lawton, M.P. 1978, "Leisure Activities for the Aged," *Annals of the American Academy of Political and Social Sciences*, 438, 71–80.

Leitner, M.J., P.L. Shepherd, and E.F. Ansello. 1980, "Recreation and the Rural Elderly," unpublished manuscript, Center on Aging, University of Maryland, College Park, Maryland.

Mortimer, I., and J. Lorence. 1979, "Work Experiences and Occupational Value Socialization: A Longitudinal Study," *American Journal Of Sociology*, 84, 1361–1385.

Moss, M., and M.P. Lawton. 1982, "Time Budgets of Older People: A Window on Four Lifestyles," *Journal Of Gerontology*, 37, 115–123.

Motley, D. 1978, "Availability of Retired Persons for Work: Findings from the Retirement History Study," *Social Security Bulletin*, 41, 18–28.

National Council on the Aging. 1975, *The Myth and Reality of Aging in America*, National Council on the Aging, Washington, D.C.

New York State Senate. 1980, *Old Age and Ruralism: A Case of Double Jeopardy, Report on the Rural Elderly*, New York State Senate, Albany, New York.

Parnes, H. 1981, *Work and Retirement: A Longitudinal Study of Men*, MIT Press, Cambridge, Massachusetts.

Pihlblad, C.T., R. Hessler, and H. Freshley. 1976, *The Rural Elderly, Eight Years Later: Changes in Life Satisfaction, Living Arrangements and Health Status*, Grant No. 93–P–57673, Administration on Aging, Washington, D.C.

Rosenfeld, C., and S. Brown. 1979, "The Labor Force Status of Older Workers," *Monthly Labor Review*, 102, 12–18.

Social Security Administration. 1976, *Reaching Retirement Age: Findings from a Survey of Newly Entitled Workers*, 1968–1970, Research Report No. 47, Social Security Administration, Washington, D.C.

Steinhauer, M.B. 1980, "Obstacles to the Mobilization and Provision of Services to the Rural Elderly," *Educational Gerontology: An International Quarterly*, 5, 399–408.

Streib, G., and C. Schneider. 1971, *Retirement in American Society*, Cornell University Press, Ithaca, N.Y.

Vinson, E.A., and F.M. Gallagher. 1980, "First Report: National Resource Committee for the Rural and Small Communities Assessment," unpublished manuscript.

Ward, R. 1984, *The Aging Experience*, Harper and Row, New York.

Weeks, J. 1984, *Aging Concepts and Issues*, Wadsworth Publishing, Belmont, California.

White House Conference on the Aging. 1981, *Chartbook on Aging in America*, White House Conference on the Aging, Washington, D.C.

Wright, J., and R. Hamilton. 1978, "Work Satisfaction and Age: Some Evidence for the 'Job Change' Hypothesis," *Social Forces*, 56, 1140–1158.

Youmans, E.G. 1962, *Leisure-time Activities of Older Persons in Selected Rural and Urban Areas of Kentucky*, Agricultural Experiment Station, University of Kentucky, Lexington, Kentucky.

Youmans, E.G., and D.K. Larson. 1977, *Health Status and Needs: A Study of Older Persons in Powell County, Kentucky*, University of Kentucky, Lexington, Kentucky.

5   PHYSICAL HEALTH

INTRODUCTION

Changes in physical health are some of the most significant aspects of the aging process. Health status is an important determinant of the elderly's behavior and life style and is also strongly related to life satisfaction among the aged (George and Bearon, 1980). Self-assessment of health, as well as objective health status, has been found to be very important in how the elderly perceive their life circumstances. Those elderly with significant health problems not only must deal with the physical and mental discomfort associated with their maladies, but they also may require costly health care. As health status worsens, the elderly must rely more on others (spouses, children, friends, and health professionals) to carry out routine activities of daily living and eventually may become restricted to spending almost all of their time at home or even face placement in a long-term care facility. Thus, the health status of the elderly raises significant issues not only for the elderly but for the health care system as well.

While the large majority of the elderly rate their health as either good or excellent compared to others their own age and while more people are living longer than ever before in the United States (White House Conference on Aging, 1981), health status generally declines as age increases. In fact, two-thirds of the elderly respondents in a national study stated that the prospect of poor health was the most dreaded aspect of growing old (National Council on the Aging, 1975), a fear that is not unjustified as over 80 percent of the 65 and over population report at least one chronic ailment, and multiple ailments are common (White House Conference on Aging, 1981). As a result, the utilization of physicians and dentists also increases with age, as do the number and length of hospital stays. Not surprisingly then, the elderly account for a disproportionately large share of total U.S. health care costs (some 30 percent) and spend considerably more on health care on a per capita basis (three times that of other age groups) (White House Conference on Aging, 1981). Two-thirds of these health care costs are born by "public sources," such as Medicare and Medicaid, at the federal, state, and local government levels (Estes et al., 1984). Thus, the provision of health care to the elderly has become a major economic and political issue in this country, and alternatives to the expensive institutional service delivery model have attracted increased attention.

These general issues set the stage for a discussion of the health status and health care needs of the rural elderly. In particular, both the objective and subjective health care status of the rural elderly and how they compare to that of the urban elderly will be examined. One objective will be to determine if the rural elderly evidence higher rates of illness and, if so, how these impact on their daily lives. It is also important to investigate rural/urban differences in how the elderly respond to their health problems and to determine the availability, accessibility, and adequacy of existing health care services. Particular attention will be paid to examining barriers to the provision of appropriate health care to the elderly who reside in rural settings.

HEALTH STATUS

Most studies of the health status of the elderly focus on reports by older people in health interviews or surveys about ailments, mobility restrictions, use of health aids, visits to doctors or dentists, or the number and length of hospital stays. By and large, self-reports of health conditions are seen by gerontologists as reliable and valid indications of the actual health status of the elderly (Maddox, 1962). There is a sizeable amount of literature available on these topics for the rural or nonmetropolitan elderly. Most of the studies do not examine national data but focus rather on small community or county samples. Nonetheless, the findings from these studies can be used to construct a picture of the rural elderly's health status.

A number of studies of the rural elderly indicate that they experience the same kind of chronic health problems as the general elderly population, including difficulties with arthritis, blood pressure, respiratory system, heart, digestive tract, sight, and hearing. The percentage of the rural elderly who report suffering from such problems varies considerably from study to study, and comparisons of findings are made difficult because of different data collection strategies. For example, Nelson (1980) reports that 87 percent of the rural elderly have a chronic illness. Preston et al. (1983) report that a 1981 study of 200 rural Pennsylvanians aged 60 and over found these chronic ailments: arthritis (64 percent), blood pressure (45 percent), respiratory (42 percent), circulation (33 percent), nerves (32 percent), heart (28 percent), eye (24 percent), bowel (23 percent), kidney (19 percent), dental (18 percent), stomach (17 percent), and diabetes (16 percent). The mean number of diseases reported was greater for those who were older or reported lower education levels. However, the percentage of those reporting a disease who indicated that the condition actually bothered them varied from 41 percent for diabetes to 91 percent for arthritis.

Similar findings are reported by Youmans and Larson (1977) for a sample of elderly Kentuckians living in towns of 2,500 or less or the open country and by Kivett and Scott (1979) for a sample of rural North Carolina elderly. Escher (1979) reported that a sample of aged-65-and-over residents of two nonmetropolitan Arizona counties noted lower rates of arthritis (49 percent) and blood pressure (28 percent), a comparable percentage for sight problems, and a higher percentage for hearing problems.

Another source of information concerning the types of ailments suffered by the rural elderly is patient records of doctors. D'Elia and Folse (1978) examined the patient records of 965 aged-60-and-over patients in 16 nonmetropolitan Illinois counties and found that a larger percentage of both general practitioners' and surgeons' patients were 65 and over (18 and 19 percent) than is the case nationally. This partly reflects the higher percentage of elderly found in rural areas. These records are consistent with the self-reports of chronic problems.

RURAL/URBAN ELDERLY HEALTH DIFFERENCES

As for rural/urban differences in the physical health status of the elderly, there are reasons to expect both better and worse health for the rural aged. On the one hand, it can be argued that rural areas have cleaner air, are less congested, and have a slower pace than urban areas. On the other hand, it can be argued that the lower incomes of the rural elderly and less adequate medical services would contribute negatively to their health (Youmans, 1967), as would their supposedly less adequate housing, transportation, and recreational opportunities (Auerbach, 1976). Without addressing the question of why such differences exist, the majority of research on reported ailments and impairments indicates the health status of the rural elderly is not as good as their urban counterparts.

In fact, one comprehensive review of the literature on rural/urban health differences has stated:

No matter what measurement of health status is used—self-assessment by the elderly individual of health as excellent, good, fair, or poor; reports of ailments; reports of mobility limitations; use of health aids or prescription drugs; number of days hospitalized; or any combination of these—the results are always the same: the rural elderly are in relatively poor health. (Ecosometrics, 1981, 94).

For example, Youmans's (1967) comparison of aged-60-and-over Kentucky men living in a rural county and a metropolitan area revealed that the rural elderly were more likely to report ailments (72 percent versus 57 percent) and that physical impairments had kept them from doing usual activities sometime in the last five years (63 percent versus 45 percent). He reported similar rural/urban differences in a later study as well (Youmans,

1974). Rural disadvantagement is also reported by Kivett and Scott (1979), Nelson (1980), Paringer et al. (1979), and Schooler (1975).

Several studies examining national or regional health statistics have also reported a higher incidence of health problems among the rural elderly. For example, McCoy and Brown (1978), in an analysis of Social Security Administration data on low income elderly, report that chronic disorders and impairments were more prevalent among the rural than the urban elderly even when sex, age, and race were statistically controlled. Focusing on a different elderly population, Dahlstein and Shank (1979) found that rural nursing home patients had a greater average number of chronic diseases than is reported nationally.

An examination of national data from the early 1960's led Ellenbogen (1967) to conclude that the health status of the rural elderly compared unfavorably to the urban on a number of indicators, including incidence of acute conditions, selected chronic conditions and impairments, and incidences of injuries or disability. Moreover, Palmore (1983), using more recent data from the National Center on Health Statistics, concludes that rural elders have more sickness and disability than the urban elderly. Burkhardt et al. (1977) also report that an analysis of 1975 vital and health statistics revealed that the rural elderly experienced more restricted mobility than the urban elderly in all regions of the country, with the largest community size differences in the South. Palmore (1983) presents national health statistics data that further reveal the farm elderly to have slightly lower rates of impairment than the nonmetropolitan nonfarm elderly.

Given such a preponderance of research findings, it would seem reasonable to assert that the rural elderly are in fact less healthy. However, the author suggests caution in accepting such a generalization without qualification. First, in most of the studies reviewed above, statistical tests are not used to determine the magnitude of the differences. That is, the findings reported may not reflect a large enough difference to be considered as significant. Without getting into a detailed discussion of statistical techniques, the question that should be asked is whether or not the reported differences are large enough to justify a conclusion that the rural elderly are less healthy. Second, as is the case in many studies of the rural/urban elderly, the definitions of "rural" and "urban" are not always stated.

For example, Palmore's (1983) report distinguishes between the "rural nonfarm" and "farm" elderly and a category labeled "all residences." The reader is not told what distinguishes rural farms from rural nonfarms. One can assume that "rural nonfarm" refers to people living in places of less than 2,500 but not on farms. A close look at the data presented by Palmore shows larger differences between the rural nonfarm and farm categories than between the rural nonfarm and all-residence categories. For some health indicators, the rural nonfarm elderly appear less healthy than the farm elderly; for others they appear more healthy. No data on the statistical significance of the differences are given.

Finally, there are studies that do not find significant rural/urban differences in the elderly's health status. The author's own work is a case in point (Krout, 1984). This study examined many aspects of 600 western New Yorkers aged 65 and over who resided in a continuum of communities: nonmetropolitan rural (less than 2,500), nonmetropolitan urban, metropolitan non–central-city, and metropolitan central city. No differences were found based on community type on a number of reported health status measures, such as number of times or days in a hospital or number of sick days, or on an overall health dependency score. This is not to suggest that the findings from this one study, or any other for that matter, provide adequate basis to reject the rural/urban difference argument.

A detailed examination of national health statistics by staff members of the Urban Institute (Paringer et al., 1979) concludes that place of residence in general is not associated with significant differences in health status. This conclusion is based on a review of data on a number of health status indicators of the elderly: mortality rates, incidence of acute illness, incidence of chronic illness, number of restricted activity days and days of bed disability, and self-assessed health. These authors find some differences based on residence, but state they are usually neither large nor consistent. The major exception was for disability days. Here it was discovered that male farm dwellers experienced the greatest number of restricted activity days. They also found some variation by geographic region, with white elderly males living in the Southeast and mining areas reporting the highest chronic illness rate for that subgroup.

The point is that much more careful and systematic research needs to be carried out before the magnitude and nature of rural/urban health status differences are clearly demonstrated. Lassey and Lassey (1985) observe that rural/urban differences in health status result from intervening factors such as lower income and the health risks and poor health care associated with it. Paringer et al. (1979) argue that more multivariate research needs to be carried out, the causal direction of variables needs to be specified, and a much greater emphasis needs to be placed on longitudinal studies.

NUTRITIONAL STATUS

It should not be surprising that diet is seen as an important component of an individual's health status and as an important factor in the course of diseases which may accompany the aging process (Kart et al., 1978). A number of studies (Krehl, 1974; Libow, 1973; Metress and Kart, 1978) have noted a significant incidence of dietary deficiencies among the elderly, especially in regard to levels of calcium, iron, and vitamins A, B, and C (Barrows and Roeder, 1977). The antecedents of such nutritional deficiencies are complex indeed and reflect the combined effects of a number of factors, such as physical illness and chronic disease, decrease in food intake quantity, qualitative deficiencies in nutrients, and various social and economic dynamics unrelated to age that inhibit the regular consumption of balanced meals (Hickey, 1980).

Although most dietary studies of the elderly focus on urban populations, a number of studies have shown that the rural elderly evidence deficiencies in specific nutrients and caloric intake similar to elderly living elsewhere (Guthrie et al., 1972; Learner and Kivett, 1981; Rawson et al., 1978). Learner and Kivett (1981) report that 11 percent of a sample of North Carolina rural elderly report frequent problems with diet, while 24 percent report some problems and 65 percent report no problems. Guthrie et al. (1972) report that between 11 and 23 percent of a sample of rural elderly had inadequate nutritional intake (depending on the measure used) and that both the low income and non–low income rural elderly had less adequate diets than the non-elderly low income.

Once again, however, some research disputes the rural elderly nutritional disadvantagement thesis. Norton and Wozny (1984) have analyzed data on nutritional adequacy for a national sample of approximately 4,000 elderly aged 60 to 74. They report no significant rural/urban difference for dietary adequacy but note that the suburban elderly do have significantly higher levels of nutrition, while the southern elderly have the lowest levels for every dietary category. These authors conclude that "residential nutritional levels are most likely due to the educational and economic status of individuals in an area and not to any causal effects of residential location" (Norton and Wozny, 1984, 592).

However, Learner and Kivett (1981) note there are indicators that suggest dietary differences based on residence. It can be argued that due to hectic public transportation and fear of crime, the city elderly may shop at local groceries that charge high prices for a limited range of goods. However, the lack of any public transportation in many rural areas may lead to infrequent shopping trips and a decreased consumption of perishable goods by the rural elderly (Rawson et al., 1978). In addition, these transportation problems may be compounded by the poorer economic conditions of rural areas. But considering the wide range of factors that affect nutritional status, it is difficult to determine the relative effect that residence per se has on this important health-related variable. Unfortunately, few rural/urban comparisons of the elderly's nutritional status are available.

SELF-ASSESSED HEALTH

Another often-used indicator of health status is an overall health self-assessment question that asks the elderly to rate their health as excellent, good, fair, or poor—either in general or compared to others their own age. Several recent national surveys have found that the majority (70 percent) of the elderly see their health as good or excellent, 20 percent see it as fair, and

10 percent as poor (Harris, 1978; U.S. Department of Health, Education and Welfare, 1977).

Some studies of the rural elderly report findings that are fairly close to these national statistics but do show the rural elderly as less likely to rate their health as good or excellent and more likely to rate it as fair or poor. Auerbach (1976) found that 80 percent of a sample of elderly living in five rural Illinois counties rated their health from fair to excellent and 20 percent as poor. Similar findings are reported for a sample of the Arizona rural elderly (Escher, 1979). However, several other studies have found a considerable proportion of the rural elderly reporting their health as poor. For example, Kivett and Scott (1979), in a study of rural North Carolina elderly that included some elderly living in group quarters, found that 29 percent of their sample saw their health as poor, while 32 percent saw it as good or excellent. Finally, Youmans and Larson (1977) report that 41 percent of a sample of aged-60-and-over rural Kentucky residents saw their health as poor—regardless of sex or age.

Not surprisingly, several studies report that the urban elderly are more likely to see their health as good or excellent than the rural elderly (Kovar, 1977; Youmans, 1967). However, two studies by the author have not found the urban elderly expressing more positive self-assessments of health. One study of some 6,000 elderly in a nonmetropolitan county found the open country and small village elderly more likely to say their health was better than the elderly living in places of 2,500 or more (Krout and Larson, 1980). A more recent study of 600 elderly living in a wide range of communities in a nonmetropolitan and metropolitan county found elderly nonmetropolitan residents most likely to say their health was better than others their same age, even when socio-demographic variables such as race, sex, income, and education were controlled for (Krout, 1984).

HEALTH CARE

Closely related to the health status of the rural elderly are several aspects of the health care system. The availability of adequate health care resources clearly can affect the health status of the elderly. In addition, the elderly's knowledge of and attitudes toward health services and professionals can affect their propensity to use such services even if availability and accessibility are not problems.

In terms of health care availability, it has been well documented that rural areas have fewer health resources and services and a lower ratio of doctors, nurses, pharmacists, and other health care personnel than do urban areas (Lipman, 1978; McCoy and Brown, 1978; Nelson, 1980; Youmans, 1974). It has also been reported that rural areas are lacking in emergency medical care (Lipman, 1978). According to Kim (1981), only 12 percent of the nation's doctors and 18 percent of the registered nurses work in nonmetropolitan places, where approximately one-third of the total population lives. In fact, Kim (1981) notes that 45 percent of the nation's medically underserved counties are nonmetropolitan and that health facilities in nonmetropolitan countries are often smaller, older, and less likely to be accredited. In addition, D'Elia and Folse (1978) concluded after an examination of the patient records of medics and surgeons located in 16 nonmetropolitan Illinois counties that the treatment of accidents and injuries in physicians' offices reflects the absence of out-patient clinics separate from emergency rooms in nonmetropolitan hospitals and the lack of neighborhood clinics. This paucity of medical professionals and facilities extends to preventive care and health maintenance (Lassey and Lassey, 1985), and there is some evidence that the rural elderly may enter long-term care institutions prematurely as a result of the lack of rural home care services (Greene, 1982).

In fact, Sheps and Bachar (1981) note that rural residents subsidize health care in urban areas. According to these authors, Part B Medicare subscribers in the most isolated rural areas of the country do not receive their proportion of contributions to the system, while metropolitan residents get their share as well as the deficits of rural areas. Rural communities realize only 72 percent of what they would receive if monies were contributed under a geographically equitable system. And Rural America (1977) notes that while half of all persons defined as poor live in rural areas, rural residents received only 25 percent of all Medicaid funds for health care to the poor.

As for accessibility, rural areas are almost totally lacking in public transportation that would enable those elderly who do not or cannot drive to reach health care facilities (Lipman, 1978; Youmans, 1977). The rural elderly themselves indicate that finding a way to get to health services is problematic. Youmans and Larson (1977) report that 31 and 21 percent of a sample of Kentucky elderly report difficulties in getting to a doctor or hospital respectively. Guthrie et al. (1972), in a study of the nutritional status of the rural elderly, found that problems of transportation were the major deterrents to the 74 percent of eligible elderly who did not take advantage of a food assistance program.

Of course, transportation problems are not the only factor that affect the rural elderly's utilization of available health care resources. Palmore (1983) has identified a number of factors that present obstacles to obtaining adequate medical care, several of which are relevant to this discussion. The first obstacle or barrier, assuming a health symptom occurs, is ignorance or denial. Palmore (1983) and Oliver (1975) argue that many rural elderly ignore or deny symptoms because of their lower education and knowledge of illnesses. While this tendency to ignore symptoms exists for all elderly regardless of residence, several authors have argued that the rural elderly have particularly strong beliefs in self-reliance (Coward, 1979) that lead them to deny they have problems (Karcher and Karcher, 1979; Moen, 1978).

Assuming the symptom is recognized, a decision must be made as to whether or not professional treatment is an appropriate response and that its benefits will outweigh the costs of obtaining such care. Oliver (1975) argues that the rural elderly are more inclined to practice self-medication and to use home remedies. He further argues that the rural elderly may mistrust doctors partly because of the disappearance of the close doctor-patient relationship due to the increased specialization of medicine and the shortage of doctors in rural areas. The strong belief in independence may also inhibit the rural elderly from seeking professional help (Karcher and Karcher, 1979).

The availability of transportation or lack of it enters here, as does the financial ability of the rural elderly to pay for medical assistance. A number of researchers have argued that the rural elderly have more limited financial resources to pay for medical care (Coward and Kerckhoff, 1978; Lassey and Lee, 1980; and

Youmans, 1977). Further, Rural America (1977) reports that the rural elderly often do not have adequate private health insurance coverage and that Medicare or Medicaid reimbursable services available in urban areas are not always available to rural populations. Another factor seen as decreasing the likelihood of medical service use by the rural elderly is their lack of awareness of existing services. The author's recent study of a sample of western New York elderly revealed that awareness of health-related services was lower for residents of a nonmetropolitan county than for residents of a neighboring metropolitan area (Krout, 1984).

OBSTACLES TO HEALTH CARE

The reasons for the under-utilization of health care by the rural elderly are numerous and complex. It should come as no surprise, then, that few simple solutions exist to this problem. Clearly, more health care facilities and professionals are needed in rural areas, and service delivery strategies must be developed that neutralize the many obstacles to the use of such services, be they related to finances, accessibility, or attitudes. Some authors note the need to develop federal health regulations that address specifically the needs of the rural elderly (Kivett and Scott, 1979). Others suggest that health services and facilities must be decentralized and brought to the rural elderly where they live. This could take the form of mobile health service units, home health services, and nurse practitioners and medical aids (Bell, 1975; National Council on Aging, 1979). Youmans and Larson (1977) further note that special facilities utilizing trained laypersons and paraprofessionals would help in this matter. The National Rural Strategy Conference (1979) has recommended a long list of strategies to overcome the shortages and inadequacies of health care to the rural aged. These major areas include:

- development of a continuum of home care involving both legislative and administrative initiatives
- provision for increased third-party reimbursement for medical/health services
- improvement of the access to medical and other health-related services

- reducing the incidence of chemical substance abuse among the rural elderly

Still other authors (Hirayama, 1979) stress the need to develop stronger health care and health maintenance programs for the chronically ill or disabled elderly. Accomplishment of such a goal would require changes in the socio-economic structure of current health care systems and in the socio-cultural characteristics of the elderly themselves. Factors to be addressed include the acute treatment orientation of U.S. health care, excessive control of health care systems by physicians, the importance of life style for health behavior, and the physical isolation of the rural elderly. Hirayama suggests the adoption of a model of primary health care developed by Brody (1973) that includes five components: personal services, supportive medical services, personal care and maintenance, counseling, and linkages.

RESEARCH NEEDS

A sizeable number of studies have been conducted on the health status of the rural elderly. Most of these have recorded self-reports of ailments, general health status, or contact with health care professionals and services. The majority of these studies have been restricted to a limited geographical area, have cross-sectional rather than longitudinal designs, have not included a range of community types in their samples, and have not used multivariate statistical techniques. It is evident, therefore, that future work must move beyond this research tradition to investigate more precisely the rural/urban differences in a large number of health status indicators of the elderly. Specifically, researchers should adopt research designs that include a wide range of communities and regions, collect data on the health care system as well as self-reported indicators of physical health status, and investigate variations based on socio-demographic characteristics.

Investigators must utilize multivariate statistical tests to determine the significance of observed rural/urban differences on health status or health care utilization and to uncover the effect of residence once other factors are taken into account. Beyond improving research designs to determine the degree of rural/ urban elderly health status differences, it is apparent that very little attention has been given to developing explanations (to say nothing of testable models) of why such differences should be expected. Very little systematic attention has been given to specifying the aspects of the rural environment that are important to understanding the elderly's health status and how these differ from urban environments. Realizing that health status is associated with a large number of inter-related factors (structural, attitudinal, and behavioral), the important question becomes how and why rural/urban residence affects these factors and health status, both directly and indirectly.

The rural disadvantagement in health care appears to have been well documented, but health care in and of itself can be expected to account for only a portion of health status. In fact, Wildovsky (1977) argues that only 10 percent of an individual's health status is affected by medical care and the other 90 percent is due to individual life style, genetics, and social conditions. Lassey and Lassey (1985), for example, note that more research needs to be done on the rural elderly's diet and nutrition and their impact on overall health status. More systematic research also is needed on how rural/urban differences in health care affect the elderly and how rural elderly health care can be improved. Lassey and Lassey (1985) further argue that research on rural/urban differences should be conducted on topics such as elderly hospital admissions and care, access to and delivery of emergency medical services, and adequacy of long-term care facilities. Special attention must be given to identifying how various factors act as barriers to health care for the rural elderly, be they barriers based on availability, accessibility, or attitudes, and on ways in which they can be overcome.

However, the basic question in need of considerably more precise attention is, To what degree and for what reasons do the rural elderly evidence significantly different health status and behaviors than the elderly residing in other community settings? The existing research, beyond demonstrating that rural/ urban health differences of an unspecified degree exist for the elderly, does not answer this question adequately.

SUMMARY

The rural elderly report many of the same kinds of physical ailments as do the elderly in general. Problems with arthritis, blood pressure, respiratory system, heart, digestive tract, sight, and hearing are most frequently mentioned. In addition, the rural elderly have been found to have deficiencies in specific nutrients and overall caloric intake. While a number of studies report the rural elderly have higher incidences of such chronic illnesses and report lower levels of overall self-assessed health than the urban elderly, the degree and nature of these differences in either overall health or specific problem areas have not been systematically investigated. The interaction of residence with other variables related to the health status and behavior of the elderly has not been adequately developed conceptually or methodologically.

Existing research has demonstrated more clearly that rural areas have fewer health professionals and facilities than urban areas and that the rural elderly are less likely to utilize available health care services. A number of factors, such as lack of accessibility due to geographic isolation, poor transportation resources, inadequate knowledge of disease or services, a high value placed on independence, and negative attitudes toward health professionals and formal medicine have been identified as related to this lack of health care use. It has been suggested, therefore, that efforts to improve the delivery of health care services to the rural elderly must proceed along multiple fronts. Greater resources must be expended to increase the number and scope of health-related services in rural areas—particularly at the federal level. Service delivery strategies such as mobile clinics must be utilized to overcome problems of accessibility, and greater resources must be placed on improving the rural elderly's health and health service awareness.

Finally, it is clear that for all the work that has been done on this topic, social scientists have yet to pay adequate attention to documenting statistical relationships between residence and health for the elderly and to developing adequate conceptual frameworks to explain these differences. It is not enough to show bivariate relationships. More effective health care policy making and planning require a more complete understanding of the complex interaction of health-related variables and residence.

REFERENCES

Auerbach, A.J. 1976, "The Elderly in Rural Areas: Differences in Urban Areas and Implications for Practice," in *Social Work in Rural Communities: A Book of Readings*, L.H. Ginsberg (ed.), Council on Social Work Education, New York.

Barrows, C., and L. Roeder. 1977, "Nutrition," in *Handbook of the Biology of Aging*, C. Finch and L. Hayflick (eds.), Van Nostrand Reinhold, New York.

Bell, B.D. 1975, "Mobile Medical Care to the Elderly: An Evaluation," *The Gerontologist*, 15, 100–103.

Brody, S. 1973, "Comprehensive Health Care for the Elderly: An Analysis," *The Gerontologist*, 13, 412–418.

Burkhardt, J.E., et al. 1977, *Techniques for Translating Units of Need Into Units of Service: The Case of Transportation and Nutrition Services for the Elderly*, prepared for the Administration on Aging, Washington, D.C.

Coward, R.T. 1979, "Planning Community Services for the Rural Elderly: Implications from Research," *The Gerontologist*, 19, 275–282.

Coward, R.T., and R.K. Kerchkhoff. 1978, *The Rural Elderly: Program Guidelines*, Iowa State University, Ames, Iowa.

Dahlstein, J., and J.C. Shank. 1979, "Chronic and Acute Disease Problems in Rural Nursing Home Patients," *Journal of the American Geriatrics Society*, 27, 112–116.

D'Elia, G., and R. Folse. 1978, "Medical Problems of the Elderly in Nonmetropolitan Illinois," *Journal of Gerontology*, 33, 681–687.

Ecosometrics. 1981, *Review of Reported Differences Between the Rural and Urban Elderly: Status, Needs, Services, and Service Costs*, final report to the Administration on Aging (Contract No. 105–80-C–056), Washington, D.C.

Ellenbogen, B.L. 1967, "Health Status of the Rural Aged," in *Older Rural Americans*, E.G. Youmans (ed.), University of Kentucky Press, Lexington, Kentucky.

Escher, M.C. 1979, "Alcohol Usage and Health Among the Rural Elderly," paper presented at the annual meeting of the Rural Sociological Society, Burlington, Vermont, August.

Estes, C., L. Gerard, J.S. Zones, and J. Swan. 1984, *Political Economy, Health, and Aging*, Little, Brown, Boston.

George, L., and L. Bearon. 1980, *Quality of Life in Older Persons: Meaning and Measurement*, Human Sciences Press, New York.

Greene, V.L. 1982, "Premature Institutionalization Among the Rural Elderly," paper presented at the Sixth Annual Institute on the Delivery of Human Services to Rural People, Jeffersonville, Vermont.

Guthrie, H.A., K. Black, and J.P. Madden. 1972, "Nutritional Practices of Elderly Citizens in Rural Pennsylvania," *The Gerontologist*, 12, 330–335.

Harris, C. 1978, *Fact Book on Aging: A Profile of America's Older Population*, National Council on the Aging, Washington, D.C.

Hickey, T. 1980, *Health and Aging*, Brooks/Cole Publishing Company, Monterey, California.

Hirayama, H. 1979, "Primary Health Care for the Rural Aged: A Model for Health Maintenance," in *Rural Aging*, D.H. Hoffman and H. Lamprey (eds.), University of Kentucky, Lexington, Kentucky.

Karcher, E.J., and B.E. Karcher. 1980, "Higher Education and Religion: Potential Partners in Service to the Rural Elderly," *Educational Gerontology: An International Quarterly*, 5, 409–421.

Kart, C., E. Metress, and J. Metress. 1978, *Aging and Health: Biological and Social Perspectives*, Addison-Wesley, Menlo Park, California.

Kim, P.K. 1981, "The Low Income Rural Elderly: Under-Served Victims of Public Inequity," in P. Kim and C. Wilson (eds.), *Toward Mental Health of the Rural Elderly*, University Press of America, Washington, D.C.

Kivett, V.R., and J.P. Scott. 1979, *The Rural By-Passed Elderly: Perspectives on Status and Needs*, Technical Bulletin No. 260, North Carolina Agricultural Research Service, University of North Carolina at Greensboro, Greensboro, North Carolina.

Kovar, M.G. 1977, "Health of the Elderly and Use of Health Services," *Public Health Reports*, 92, 9–19.

Krehl, W.A. 1974, "The Influence of Nutritional Environment on Aging," *Geriatrics*, 29, 275–277.

Krout, J.A. 1984, *The Utilization of Formal and Informal Support of the Aged: Rural Versus Urban Differences*, final report to the Andrus Foundation, American Association of Retired Persons, Fredonia, New York.

Krout, J.A., and D. Larson. 1980, "Self-Assessed Needs of the Rural Elderly," paper presented at the annual meeting of the Rural Sociological Society, Ithaca, New York.

Lassey, W.R. and M.L. Lassey. 1985, "The Physical Health Status of the Rural Elderly," in *The Elderly in Rural Society*, R. Coward and G. Lee (eds.), Springer, New York.

Lassey, W., and G. Lee. 1980, "Elderly People in Rural America," in *Research and Public Service with the Rural Elderly*, W. Lassey, M. Lassey, and G. Lee (eds.), Western Rural Development Center, Oregon State University, Corvallis, Oregon.

Learner, R.M., and V.R. Kivett. 1981, "Discriminators of Perceived Dietary Adequacy Among the Rural Elderly," *Geriatrics*, 78, 330–337.

Libow, L. 1973, "Pseudo-Senility: Acute and Reversible Organic Brain Syndrome," *Journal of the American Geriatrics Society*, 21, 112–120.

Lipman, A. 1978, *Needs Inconsistencies of the Rural Aged, Proceedings of the Workshop on Rural Gerontology, Research in the Northeast*, May 24–27, 1977, Cornell University, Ithaca, New York.

McCoy, J., and D. Brown. 1978, "Health Status Among Low-Income Elderly Persons: Rural/Urban Differences," *Social Security Bulletin*, 41, 14–26.

Maddox, G.L. 1962, "Some Correlates of Differences in Self-Assessments of Health Status Among the Elderly," *Journal of Gerontology*, 17, 180–185.

Metress, S., and C. Kart. 1978, "A System for Observing the Potential Nutritional Risks of Elderly People at Home," *Journal of Geriatric Psychiatry*, 11, 67–73.

Moen, E. 1978, "The Reluctance of the Elderly to Accept Help," *Social Problems*, 25, 293–303.

National Council on the Aging. 1979, *NCOA Public Policy Agenda: 1979–1980*, National Council on the Aging, Washington, D.C.

National Rural Strategy Conference. 1979, *Improving Services for the Rural Elderly*, National Strategy Conference on Improving Service Delivery to the Rural Elderly, Des Moines, Iowa.

Nelson, G. 1980, "Social Services to the Urban and Rural Aged: The Experience of Area Agencies on Aging," *The Gerontologist*, 20, 200–207.

Norton, L., and M.C. Wozny. 1984, "Residential Location and Nutritional Adequacy Among Elderly Adults," *Journal Of Gerontology*, 39, 592–595.

Oliver, D.B. 1975, "Nutrition and Health Care," in *Rural Environments And Aging*, R.C. Atchley and T.O. Byerts (eds.), Gerontological Society, Washington, D.C.

Palmore, E. 1983, "Health Care Needs of the Rural Elderly," *International Journal of Aging and Human Development*, 18, 39–45.

Paringer, L., J. Black, J. Feder, and J. Holahan. 1979, *Health Status and Use of Medical Services: Evidence on the Poor, the Black, and the Rural Elderly*, Urban Institute, Washington, D.C.

Preston, D.B., P.K. Mansfield, and C.D. Crawford. 1983, "Health Status, Stress, and Coping Patterns in a Sample of Rural Elderly in Central Pennsylvania," paper presented at the Second Annual Blueprints Conference: Promoting Healthful Aging, Philadelphia.

Rawson, I.G., E.I.W. Weinberg, J. Herold, and J. Holtz. 1978, "Nutrition of Rural Elderly in South-Western Pennsylvania," *The Gerontologist*, 18, 24–29.

Rural America. 1977, *Rural America Factsheet: The Elderly*, Rural America, Washington, D.C.

Schooler, K. 1975, "A Comparison of Rural and Non-Rural Elderly on Selected Variables," in *Rural Environments And Aging*, R. Atchley and T.O. Byerts (eds.), Gerontological Society, Washington, D.C.

Sheps, C.G., and M. Bachar. 1981, "Rural Areas and Personal Health Services: Current Strategies," *American Journal Of Public Health*, 71, 71–82.

U.S. Department of Health, Education, and Welfare. 1977, *First Annual Report to Congress on Title XX of the Social Security Act*, U.S. Government Printing Office, Washington, D.C.

White House Conference on Aging. 1981, *Chartbook on Aging in America*, White House Conference on Aging, Washington, D.C.

Wildovsky, A. 1977, "Doing Better and Feeling Worse: The Political Pathology of Health Policy," in *Doing Better And Feeling Worse: Health in the United States*, J.H. Knowles (ed.), W.W. Norton and Co., New York.

Youmans, E.G. 1967, "Health Orientations of Older Rural and Urban Men," *Geriatrics*, 22, 139–147.

———. 1974, "Age Group, Health, and Attitudes," *The Gerontologist*, 14, 249–254.

Youmans, E.G., and D. Larson. 1977, *Problems of Rural Elderly Households in Powell County, Kentucky*, Economic Development Division, Economics, Statistics and Cooperative Services, U.S. Department of Agriculture, Washington, D.C.

6   MENTAL HEALTH

INTRODUCTION

Gerontologists have paid a considerable amount of attention to the mental health status of the elderly as it is manifested in various mental problems, such as organic and functional disorders and suicide. In addition, much research has been carried out on the general emotional well-being or life satisfaction of the elderly. Mental health is seen as being closely related to physical health and the degree to which the elderly cope successfully with the myriad of conditions and changes that accompany normal aging.

Unfortunately, the term "mental health" is extremely ambiguous in regard to both what it is and how it should be measured. Gerontologists are not in agreement as to the appropriateness and usefulness of age-specific criteria in the determination of the elderly's mental health (Birren and Renner, 1981; Rosow, 1981). Some researchers even suggest that considerations of mental health and more subjective constructs such as life satisfaction and morale should be replaced by a focus on mental illness, which they say can be more clearly defined (Rosow, 1981). Scheidt (1985) notes that these ambiguities create difficulties for the interpretation and comparison of research findings on the elderly.

Research indicates that the incidence of mental problems increases with age, primarily as a result of increases in depression and organic brain disorders (problems with memory, learning, speech or orientation) (Ward, 1984). The percentage of the elderly affected by mental problems can only be estimated. Butler and Lewis (1982) state that at least 15 percent of the elderly are in need of mental health services. Pfeiffer (1977) also argues that 15 percent of the elderly suffer from significant or at least moderate psycho-pathology, while the White House Conference on Aging (1981) estimates that from 15 to 25 percent of the elderly have significant symptoms of mental illness.

It is generally recognized that depression is the most common mental health problem of the elderly, while other functional disorders such as paranoia, hypochondriasis, and anxiety are also important (Pfeiffer, 1977; Ward, 1984). Many of these are seen as a result of aging, and Butler and Lewis (1982) argue that loss (of spouse, social roles, economic status, physical well-being) is a significant aspect of the emotional experiences of older people. Some disorders, such as schizophrenia and manic depression, generally are carried over from the younger years. In addition, perhaps as many as one-half of the elderly with mental impairments are afflicted with organic brain syndromes—diseases of the brain cells. (Pfeiffer, 1977; Soldo, 1980). Both functional and organic disorders generally increase with age and also are more prevalent for those elderly who are in poorer physical health and not married.

While some attention has been paid to the mental health and illness of rural populations (Keller and Murray, 1982; Kim and Lamprey, 1979; Poole, 1981), few researchers have examined the interaction between age and community size (Scheidt, 1985). This chapter focuses on a number of aspects of the mental health status of the rural elderly. More specifically, it examines rural/urban differences in the types of mental disorders that affect the elderly, rural/urban differences in reported levels of the elderly's life satisfaction and morale, availability and appropriateness of mental health services for the elderly, and gaps in the existing literature on these topics.

MENTAL HEALTH STATUS OF RURAL POPULATIONS

Very little research is available on the relationship between residence and rates of specific functional or organic mental problems of the elderly. It can be argued that the rural elderly should evidence higher rates of these problems because of their supposed lower income and health levels—two factors known to be related to emotional well-being (Flax et al., 1979; Youmans, 1977). In addition, the lack of health care professionals and facilities documented in the previous chapter would suggest that the rural elderly may suffer additional stress due to untreated medical conditions.

On the other hand, a number of influential sociologists have argued that the relative simplicity and traditional basis of rural life produces less stress than the complex, hectic, big-city environment (Durkheim, 1951; Srole, 1978). Recall Wirth's (1936) classic argument that the size, density, and heterogeneity of the modern metropolis lead to higher rates of social and individual pathologies such as mental illness. Others have argued that "crowding," presumably greater in cities, leads to increased levels of alienation and even pathology (Freedman, 1975).

The fact is that an adequate research base on mental health disorders in rural areas in general, and the elderly in particular, simply does not exist. Rural samples are usually not used, and lack of uniformity in definition, data collection, and data analysis makes a comparison of existing data risky at best. In fact, one researcher has gone so far as to state, "Given the differences in concepts and methods used in identifying cases in the true prevalence studies, comparisons of rate differences across studies done in rural and urban settings by different investigators is an exercise in futility" (Dohrenwend, 1977, 58). Studies also reveal tremendous variation within community types. Dohrenwend and Dohrenwend (1965) reviewed a number of studies on treated and untreated mental disorders and found rates in urban areas ranging from 2 to 32 percent and from 2 to 64 percent in rural places.

Research findings do not support an unequivocal answer to the question of rural/urban differences in mental illness rates. Link and Dohrenwend (1980) report that a Florida study found higher rates of untreated, but lower rates of treated, mental disorders for rural areas. However, a study with national data reviewed by these authors found very small differences based on community type. Srole (1978) reports higher rates of mental disorders in Manhattan versus rural Nova Scotia. One comprehensive review of rural mental health notes that rural populations have higher rates of psychoses, while city populations have higher rates of neuroses and personality disorders (Flax et al., 1979). Indeed, these authors are willing to advance a "working" hypothesis that rural areas are characterized by a greater prevalence of mental disorders but qualify this position by noting that "more epidemiological investigations using appropriately matched study sites and controlling for their diagnostic and methodological problems are needed" (Flax et al., 1979, 26). While their review was not specific to the elderly, their reservations are well taken. Another comprehensive review by Mueller (1981) found that the results from different studies yielded inconsistent findings as to rural/urban differences on mental disorder rates.

ELDERLY MENTAL DISORDERS AND RESIDENCE

While there has not been a sizeable amount of research on rural/urban differences in mental disorders of the elderly, a few studies have been conducted on this topic that are of interest. In general, they do not support clear rural/urban differences but rather underscore the difficulty in determining the impact of residence on mental status. For example, Schwab et al. (1974), in a study of psychiatric disorders among Florida residents, conclude that "simple rural-urban comparisons of mental illness rates are relatively meaningless in view of the evidence which shows clearly that psychiatric disorder is associated with low incomes and deprivation while health is associated with relative affluence and opportunity" (Schwab et al., 1974, 274). In another study, Comstock and Helsing (1976) interviewed residents of Kansas City and a Maryland county to ascertain symptoms of clinical depression and found no rural/urban differences. They argue that comparing populations on rates of mental disorder is valid only if the populations have similar characteristics.

It should also be noted that comparisons of the rural elderly to the urban elderly on rates of various mental illness are confounded by other factors as well. The shortage of appropriate treatment facilities and mental health professionals in rural areas may result in the rural elderly seeking treatment in urban places, thus artificially increasing the urban rates. In addition, differences in rates of mental health service utilization by residence may also reflect differences in the likelihood that the elderly are able and/or willing to identify and/or admit to symptoms of mental problems and to see them as in need of professional treatment. The determination of the actual rates of mental problems in the rural or urban elderly, then, becomes exceedingly difficult as one tries to sort out the influences of differences in general values, attitudes toward health and health care, and service delivery systems, to name just a few.

LIFE SATISFACTION OF THE RURAL ELDERLY

A considerable amount of research is available on more generalized measures of the elderly's mental health such as life satisfaction. "Life satisfaction" is a global term that incorporates concepts such as happiness, morale, and self-esteem. The elderly overall express life satisfaction levels that are comparable to the general population (National Council on the Aging, 1975; Weeks, 1984). For example, Weeks (1984) reports that 42 percent of the elderly respondents in a 1977 national sample said they were "very happy," while 36 percent of those 45–64 noted the same, and fully 87 percent of the elderly in another national survey agreed that they were fairly well satisfied in looking back on their life, while 57 percent indicated they expected enjoyable things to happen to them in the future (National Council on the Aging, 1975). Life satisfaction levels in general are higher for those elderly who are healthier, wealthier, better educated, and more active (Marksides and Martin, 1979; Palmore and Luikart, 1972; Seleen, 1982), although Cutler (1979) notes that the things from which people get satisfaction may shift with age.

Most life satisfaction studies have not systematically examined the impact of residence (Powers, Keith, and Goudy, 1977), although there is a small amount of literature on rural/urban differences on this topic. It can be argued, on the one hand, that the supposed disadvantaged status of the rural elderly in areas such as health, income, housing, transportation, and services should be reflected in lower levels of life satisfaction and morale (Youmans, 1977). This line of argument can be reinforced by the observation that the low population densities of rural areas lead to a greater isolation of the rural elderly from their relatives and friends, which would reduce life satisfaction (Donnenwerth et al., 1978). Bultena (1969) reports that the urban elderly have more interaction with their children than do the rural elderly, and the author's recent study of 600 western New York elderly also found that in-person contact with children increased with the size of the community (Krout, 1984).

Several studies do report that rural elderly samples express lower levels of life satisfaction or morale than urban samples. Shook (1980) reports this in a study comparing the urban elderly in Cleveland, Ohio, and Oregon to the rural elderly in Oregon and Kentucky, as does Youmans (1961) for rural and metropolitan samples of Kentucky elderly. Further, a large national interview survey by Schooler (1975) found persons aged 65 and over living in rural areas more likely to exhibit greater alienation and lower morale than the urban elderly. These differences generally held up when demographic differences were controlled for and when a follow-up study was conducted three years later. However, a careful review of the available research on rural/urban differences on elderly life satisfaction suggests that no consistent or strong impact of residence per se has been established and that the introduction of controls for traditional sociodemographic or health measures substantially alters observed bivariate relationships.

Several studies report higher levels of life satisfaction among the rural elderly. Donnenwerth et al. (1978) report that rural residence has a small positive effect on life satisfaction, primarily because of higher levels of social contact among the rural elderly. Edwards and Klemmack (1973), although finding no bivariate relationship between residence and morale, note an inverse relationship between these two variables when controlling for other factors. Yet some studies report finding no relationship between residence and life satisfaction (Lawton et al., 1975; Pihlblad and Rosencranz, 1969), while others report that the nature of the relationship depends on the measure of well-being that is used (Schooler, 1975; Youmans, 1977).

The necessity and importance of controlling for other variables is well illustrated in a study by Hynson (1975). He examined data from a national sample and found the rural elderly generally reported themselves to be happier than the urban elderly. The data came from the National Opinion Center for those aged 60 and over and were broken down into three residence categories: less than 2,500, 2,500–250,000, and greater than 250,000. Respondents were asked how satisfied they were with family and community, whether they were generally happy, and whether they were afraid to go out into the community. All of these measures of satisfaction increased as community size decreased except for satisfaction with family. No statistical controls were introduced. Hynson (1975) argued these differences probably reflected the greater sense of community and level of social integration in rural areas. Sauer et al. (1976) examined the same data in a multivariate framework and demonstrated that the effect of residence disappeared when variables such as race, sex, marital status, employment status, and socio-economic status were controlled for.

However, it should be noted that Sauer et al. (1976) used an overall composite measure of life satisfaction, while Hynson (1975) used four separate measures, and as Lee (1981) points out, the Sauer et al. (1976) finding does not demonstrate that residence is unrelated to life satisfaction but rather that the *direct* effect is not significant. Residence may, however, have an intervening effect on life satisfaction. Lee's (1981) own multivariate analysis with data from the state of Washington shows that residence has a positive indirect effect and a negative direct effect on morale of the elderly. The result is a negligible total effect with very little explanatory value. Lee (1981) observes that the expected negative impact of rural residence on the elderly's life satisfaction in his and other studies may result from the fact that the antecedents of life satisfaction differ in kind or degree in different locations or that rural advantages exist that offset the disadvantages. However, several studies (Harel et al., 1982; Kivett and Learner, 1982) have shown that the correlates of life satisfaction among the rural elderly are similar to those for the elderly in general.

Several researchers have gone beyond simply uncovering rural/urban differences in levels of elderly life satisfaction to identifying the importance various factors play in explaining or predicting life satisfaction. Fengler and Jensen (1981) examined predictors of life satisfaction for a sample of Vermont elderly. They found that predictors such as self-perceived income, perceived problems in getting access to transportation, and organization participation were stronger determinants of life satisfaction for the urban as opposed to the nonurban elderly. Another study focused on the impact of perceived physical and psychological community attributes on the psychological well-being of Kansas elderly living in towns of 2,500 and less. The results of this research have been reported in a number of articles (Scheidt, 1981; Scheidt and Windley, 1982; Windley and Scheidt, 1980, 1982). Satisfaction with one's dwelling features (lighting, temperature, adequacy of space), house and neighborhood quality, and the number of reported social and physical barriers to participation in town activities were found to be positively related to mental health (Scheidt and Windley, 1982). Even though the authors report that these and several other variables accounted for only 17 percent of the variation in mental health scores and their sample does not allow for a rural/urban comparison, this research strikes out in a needed direction.

MENTAL HEALTH SERVICES FOR THE RURAL ELDERLY

Despite the elderly's apparent greater risk of suffering from significant mental health problems, it appears that they are under-represented when it comes to mental health service utilization (Redick and Taube, 1980; Ward, 1984; White House Conference on Aging, 1981). For example, the White House Conference on Aging (1981) reports that the elderly account for only 5 percent of the total admissions to state and county hospitals and 3 to 4 percent of admissions to mental health clinics and out-patient psychiatric care facilities. Thus, as Redick and Taube (1980) point out, a relatively small percentage of the elderly with mental health problems are using mental health services.

As for mental health services for the rural elderly, it is not surprising to find that few are available (Kim, 1981). The New York State Senate (1980) reports that the rural elderly are less likely to have access to such services and that custodial care for the severely mentally disturbed is especially scarce. Once more, federally supported mental health services in rural areas are seen as less adequate (Kim, 1981), a finding that should not be surprising as data from the late 1970's indicate that only 14 percent of the federal outlays in mental health were in rural areas.

Flax et al. (1979) review a large number of barriers to the delivery of mental health services in rural areas that presumably affect the elderly. These include the attitudes and values of clients, the delivery models used by service providers, and the lack of psychiatric facilities in general hospitals and out-patient facilities. These authors note that values affect the ways in which the rural elderly respond to problems and their propensity to utilize mental health services. These values also have implications for intervention and mental health service delivery strategies as well. Hargrove (1982), for example, points out how rural community mental health professionals must be careful to recognize (and use to their advantage) the unique cultural and organizational characteristics of rural areas. They must work to fit in with and be accepted by the local population.

Perhaps even more basic to the problem is the overall lack of funding for mental health treatment, especially out-patient services (Lowy, 1980). This dollar problem is no doubt related to the critical shortage of mental health professionals with training aimed specifically at treating elderly individuals. It is clear that additional financial resources (especially federal) could be used to increase the availability and accessibility of mental health services and professionals to the rural elderly. The New York State Senate report (1980) argues that the community mental health system in rural areas needs to be significantly strengthened.

RESEARCH NEEDS

Much research needs to be carried out on many aspects of the mental health status of the rural elderly. Very little data on the rates of functional and mental problems experienced by the elderly living outside metropolitan areas are available. Thus, more attention needs to be given to collecting and analyzing data on mental health problems of the elderly as they differ by residence.

Differences in data collection methods and definitions of "treated" versus "untreated" disorders make comparisons of data from existing studies very difficult. In addition, data available from health care facilities provide only a partial picture, as few such facilities are located in rural areas and the rural elderly, even more so than the urban elderly, may be unlikely to use what is available. Thus, there is a need for extensive field studies to collect this information.

Very little is known of the specific factors that affect the mental health of the rural elderly or how they operate. While it is often observed that there are differences in the economic status, physical health, housing, values, and social interaction patterns of the rural elderly, the way in which these factors affect mental health status either indirectly or directly has received inadequate conceptual and empirical attention. And while more attention has been given to the question of life satisfaction or morale, the inconsistent and often contradictory findings on this topic reviewed earlier underscore the need for tighter research designs and more replication studies. Mental health status is a complex phenomenon with multiple antecedents, yet research on the rural elderly has yielded few insights on this topic. Perhaps as much as any other substantive area of gerontological research, the work on mental health demonstrates how much more rigor needs to be brought to the examination of the causal impact of the rural elderly's environment and the characteristics of rural populations.

In addition, the limitations and strengths of rural areas in meeting the mental health needs of the rural elderly must be examined much more carefully. It would appear that the present mental health care system is not sufficient to meet the demand, to say nothing of the need for such care among the rural elderly. The literature has identified a number of barriers to the delivery of mental health services in rural areas. But how these and other perhaps less well identified factors operate and how they might be most appropriately and successfully overcome has not been well investigated. Most of the emphasis in this regard has been placed on physical health care services (see Chapter 5), and while some strategies in this area may be appropriate for mental health, others may miss the mark entirely. Greater financial and human resources need to be committed to addressing the mental health needs of the rural elderly, but additional research is critical to determining how those resources can and should be best applied.

SUMMARY

It is evident from the materials reviewed in this chapter that despite the importance of mental health in the lives of the elderly, many questions remain unresolved in regard to this phenomenon. Researchers do not agree on how this concept is most appropriately conceptualized or measured. As a result, the magnitude and nature of mental health disorders among the elderly in general, and the rural elderly in particular, are not well documented. Part of this knowledge gap concerning the rural elderly is due to the lack of attention given mental health/disorder differences based on residence for the general population. A review of research indicates an extremely wide range of treated and untreated mental disorder rates within and between rural and urban samples. And the few studies that have focused on rural/urban differences in mental disorders of the elderly have not produced consistent findings or conclusions. In fact, existing studies point over and over again to the difficulties in identifying residence differences in the mental illness or wellness of the elderly.

Considerable attention has been devoted by gerontologists to a concept also linked to mental health—life satisfaction. Most studies report that the elderly express life satisfaction levels comparable to the general population. Some attention has been paid to rural/urban differences in elderly life satisfaction, with arguments put forth for both a rural advantage and disadvantage. Once again, research findings do not support either hypothesis. Thus, while some studies do show rural/urban differences, the findings are not consistent and lead to the conclusion that such variations based on residence are not clearly supported by empirical evidence.

Little doubt exists regarding the rural disadvantage in terms of mental health services for the elderly, however. Rural areas face resource shortfalls in terms of dollars, personnel, and facilities that are compounded by problems of access and the value systems of rural places and people. It has been demonstrated that federal outlays for rural mental health services in particular are not proportional in terms of either population or need.

Not surprisingly, this chapter has noted that gaps exist in the literature on the mental health of the rural elderly. There is simply too little information available on this topic. The quality of the data that has been collected suffers from conceptual and operational weaknesses that plague discussions of mental health in general. In addition, little is known about how various aspects of the rural environment affect the mental health of the elderly directly or indirectly. While some research has been conducted on life satisfaction levels of the rural elderly, it has been largely descriptive. Finally, it is clear that the formal mental health service structure in rural areas is not adequate to meet the needs of the elderly. Unfortunately, little attention has been given to developing and evaluating service delivery strategies that overcome the weaknesses of the existing system (or lack of system) and improve the quantity and quality of mental health assistance to the rural elderly.

REFERENCES

Birren, J.E., and V.J Renner. 1981, "Concepts and Criteria of Mental Health and Aging," *American Journal of Orthopsychiatry*, 51, 242–254.

Bultena, G. 1969, "Rural-Urban Differences in the Familial Interaction of the Aged," *Rural Sociology*, 34, 5–15.

Butler, R., and M. Lewis. 1982, *Aging and Mental Health: Positive Psychosocial Approaches*, C.V. Mosley, St. Louis.

Comstock, G.W., and K.J. Helsing. 1976, "Symptoms of Depression in Two Communities," *Psychological Medicine*, 6, 551–563.

Cutler, N. 1979, "Age Variations in the Dimensionality of Life Satisfaction," *Journal of Gerontology*, 34, 573–578.

Dohrenwend, B.P. 1977, "The Epidemiology of Mental Illness: Psychiatric Epidemiology as a Knowledge Base for Primary Prevention in Community Psychiatry and Community Mental Health," in *New Trends in Psychiatry in the Community*, G. Serban and B. Astrachan (eds.), Ballinger, Cambridge, Massachusetts.

Dohrenwend, B.P., and B.S. Dohrenwend. 1965, "The Problem of Validity in Field Studies of Psychological Disorder," *Journal of Abnormal Psychology*, 70, 52–59.

Donnenwerth, G., R. Guy, and M. Norvell. 1978, "Life Satisfaction Among Older Persons: Rural-Urban and Racial Comparisons," *Social Science Quarterly*, 59, 578–583.

Durkheim, E. 1951, *Suicide: A Study in Sociology*, J. Spaulding and G. Simpson, (trans.), Free Press, New York.

Edwards, J., and D. Klemmoch. 1973, "Correlates of Life Satisfaction: A Re-examination," *Journal of Gerontology*, 28, 497–502.

Fengler, A.P., and L. Jensen. 1981, "Perceived and Objective Conditions as Predictors of the Life-Satisfaction of Urban and Nonurban Elderly," *Journal of Gerontology*, 36, 750–752.

Flax, J.W., M. Wagenfeld, R. Ivens, and R.J. Weiss. 1979, *Mental Health and Rural America: An Overview and Annotated Bibliography*, U.S. Department of Health, Education, and Welfare, Washington, D.C.

Freedman, J. 1975, *Crowding and Behavior*, Freeman, San Francisco.

Harel, Z., R.N. Sollod, and B.J. Bognar. 1982, "Predictors of Mental Health Among Semi Rural Aged," *The Gerontologist*, 22, 499–504.

Hargrove, D.S. 1982, "An Overview of Professional Considerations in the Rural Community," in *Handbook of Rural Community Mental Health*," P.A. Keller and J.D. Murray (eds.), Human Sciences Press, New York.

Hynson, L. 1975, "Rural-Urban Differences in Satisfaction Among the Elderly," *Rural Sociology*, 40, 64–66.

Keller, P.A., and J.D. Murray. 1982, *Handbook of Rural Community Mental Health*, Human Sciences Press, New York.

Kim, P.K., 1981, "The Low Income Rural Elderly: Under-Served Victims of Public Inequity," in *Toward Mental Health of the Rural Elderly*, P. Kim and C. Wilson (eds.), University Press of America, Washington, D.C.

Kim, P.K., and H. Lamprey. 1979, *A Bibliography on Aspects of Mental Health in Rural Aging*, Gerontology Publication Series No. 1979–1, University of Kentucky, Lexington, Kentucky.

Kivett, V., and R. Learner. 1982, "Situational Influences on the Morale of Older Rural Adults in Child-Shared Housing: A Comparative Analysis," *The Gerontologist*, 22, 100–106.

Krout, J.A. 1984, *The Utilization of Formal and Informal Support of the Aged: Rural Versus Urban Differences*, final report to the Andrus Foundation, American Association of Retired Persons, Fredonia, New York.

Lawton, M.P., L. Nahemow, and J. Teaff. 1975, "Housing Characteristics and the Well-Being of Elderly Tenants in Federally Assisted Housing," *Journal of Gerontology*, 30, 601–607.

Lee, G. 1981, "Rural-Urban Residence and Emotional Well-Being Among the Elderly," paper presented at the annual meeting of the Rural Sociological Society, Guelph, Ontario.

Link, B., and B.P. Dohrenwend. 1980, "Formulation of Hypotheses About the True Prevalence of Demoralization in the United States," in *Mental Illness in the United States: Epidemiological Estimates*, B.L. Dohrenwend et al. (eds.), Praeger, New York.

Lowy, L. 1980, *Social Policies and Programs on Aging*, Lexington Books, Lexington, Massachusetts.

Marksides, K., and H. Martin. 1979, "A Causal Model of Life Satisfaction Among the Elderly," *Journal of Gerontology*, 34, 86–93.

Mueller, D.P. 1981, "The Current Status of Urban-Rural Differences in Psychiatric Disorder," *Journal of Nervous and Mental Disease*, 169, 18–27.

National Council on the Aging. 1975, *The Myths and Reality of Aging*, National Council on the Aging, Washington, D.C.

New York State Senate. 1980, *Old Age and Ruralism: A Case of Double Jeopardy, Report on the Rural Elderly*, New York State Senate, Albany, New York.

Palmore, E., and C. Luikart. 1972, "Health and Social Factors Related to Life Satisfaction," *Journal of Health and Social Behavior*, 13, 68–80.

Pfeiffer, E. 1977, "Psychopathology and Social Pathology," in *Handbook of Psychology of Aging*, J. Birren and K.W. Schaie (eds.), Van Nostrand Reinhold, New York.

Pihlblad, C., and H. Rosencranz. 1969, *Social Adjustment of Older People in the Small Town*, Department of Sociology, University of Missouri, Columbia, Missouri.

Poole, D.L. 1981, *Rural Social Welfare: An Annotated Bibliography for Educators and Practitioners*, Praeger, New York.

Powers, E.A., P.M. Keith, and W.J. Goudy. 1977, *Later Life Transitions: Older Males in Rural America*, Sociology Report No. 139, Iowa State University, Ames, Iowa.

Redick, R., and C. Taube. 1980, "Demography and Mental Health Care of the Aged," in *Handbook of Mental Health and Aging*, J. Birren and R. Sloane (eds.), Prentice-Hall, Englewood Cliffs, New Jersey.

Rosow, I. 1981, "DOCS: Ortho and Para," *American Journal of Orthopsychiatry*, 51, 225–59.

Sauer, W., C. Shehan, and C. Boymel. 1976, "Rural-Urban Differences in Satisfaction Among the Elderly: A Reconsideration," *Rural Sociology*, 41, 269–275.

Scheidt, R.J. 1981, "Psychosocial Environmental Predictors of the Mental Health of Small Town Rural Elderly," in *Toward Mental Health of the Rural Elderly*, P. Kim and C. Wilson (eds.), University Press of America, Washington, D.C.

————. 1985, "The Mental Health of the Aged in Rural Environments," in *The Elderly in Rural Society*, R. Coward and G. Lee (eds.), Springer, New York.

Scheidt, R.J., and P.G. Windley. 1982, "Well-Being Profiles of Small-Town Elderly in Differing Rural Contexts," *Community Mental Health Journal*, 18, 257–267.

Schooler, K. 1975, "A Comparison of Rural and Non-Rural Elderly on Selected Variables," in *Rural Environments and Aging*, R. Atchley and T.O. Byerts (eds.), Gerontological Society, Washington, D.C.

Schwab, J., G. Warheit, and C. Halzer. 1974, "Mental Health: Rural Urban Comparisons," *Mental Health and Society*, 1, 265–274.

Seleen, D. 1982, "The Congruence Between Actual and Desired Use of Time by Older Adults: A Predictor of Life Satisfaction," *The Gerontologist*, 22, 95–99.

Shook, W. 1980, "Urban and Rural Older People: Their Well-Being and Needs," paper presented at the annual meeting of the Gerontological Society of America, San Diego, California, November.

Soldo, B. 1980, "America's Elderly in the 1980's," *Population Bulletin*, 35, 1–47.

Srole, L. 1978, "The City Versus Town and Country: New Evidence on an Ancient Bias, 1975," in *Mental Health in the Metropolis: The Midtown Manhattan Study*, L. Srole and A.K. Fisher (eds.), New York University Press, New York.

Ward, R. 1984, *The Aging Experience: An Introduction to Social Gerontology*, Harper and Row, New York.

Weeks, J.R. 1984, *Aging: Concepts and Social Issues*, Wadsworth Publishing, Belmont, California.

White House Conference on Aging. 1981, *Chartbook on Aging in America*, White House Conference on Aging, Washington, D.C.

Windley, P.G., and R.R. Scheidt. 1980, "The Well-Being of Older Persons in Small Rural Towns: A Town Panel Approach," *Educational Gerontology*, 5, 355–373.

————. 1982, "An Ecological Model of the Mental Health Among Small-Town Rural Elderly," *Journal of Gerontology*, 37, 235–242.

Wirth, L. 1936, "Urbanism as a Way of Life," *American Journal of Sociology*, 44, 3–24.

Youmans, E.G. 1961, "Pessimism Among Older Rural and Urban Persons," *Journal of Health and Human Behavior*, 2, 132–137.

————. 1977, The Rural Aged, *Annals of the American Academy of Political Science*, 429, 81–90.

7   HOUSING AND
TRANSPORTATION

INTRODUCTION

Both of the topics considered in this chapter are of great importance for the elderly in general and the rural elderly in particular. Housing provides the immediate setting in which one lives and gains protection from the environment, and its cost and adequacy can have substantial impacts on other aspects of daily life. As people age, they may become less mobile because of health problems and reduced income and thus spend more and more time at home. However, their homes age as well, and what was once a comfortable and functional domicile may no longer be appropriate for the capabilities or financial resources of the elderly person. The home represents a great economic and emotional investment, and the elderly often desire to remain living there independently as long as possible. In fact, about 85–90 percent of all elderly live independently in their own homes (Ward, 1984).

It should come as no surprise that many aspects of the housing status of the elderly have drawn considerable attention from gerontologists. However, relatively few researchers have focused on the housing situation of the rural elderly. This chapter reviews the existing literature on rural housing and specifically addresses the following topics: home ownership and cost, housing quality, housing satisfaction, and housing programs. Suggestions for future research are also discussed.

Transportation is an equally important aspect of many people's lives. Modern America's economy and society are heavily dependent on the ability of people to move about freely by means of the private automobile. Access to affordable and appropriate transportation is crucial for people to participate fully in economic, social, and recreational activities (Carp, 1979). In addition, adequate transportation contributes to the morale and life satisfaction of the elderly (Berghorn et al., 1978; Cutler, 1975; Fengler and Danigelis, 1982; Kivett and Scott, 1979).

Transportation problems can be particularly acute for the elderly, who are less likely than younger people to own or be able to operate their own car (McGhee, 1983). According to the 1981 White House Conference on the Aging, elderly-headed households are twice as likely not to own a car. Thus, the elderly are more likely to experience difficulties in visiting others, shopping for life's necessities, or utilizing needed social or medical services even as their need for such services increases (Ward, 1984). The elderly see difficulties with transportation as one of the biggest problems they face, if not the biggest (Ecosometrics, 1981; White House Conference on Aging, 1981). This problem is even greater for the elderly living in rural areas, where distances between people and services are greater and where lower population densities have made the cost of public transportation prohibitive (Kaye, 1978; Lassey et al., 1980; McGhee, 1983).

This chapter will examine what is known about the transportation status of the rural elderly and specifically addresses these topics: availability of personal and public transportation, transportation satisfaction and problems, and transportation programs. Areas in need of further study are outlined and a chapter summary reviews both the transportation and housing of the rural elderly.

HOME OWNERSHIP

Not surprisingly, the elderly in general are more likely to own their homes than younger people (Weeks, 1984). National data from the mid 1970's indicate that 70 percent of elderly household heads own their homes versus 60 percent of non-elderly house-hold heads (White House Conference on Aging, 1981). The elderly are also much more likely than the non-elderly to own their homes mortgage-free (almost three times as likely) (White House Conference on Aging, 1981). Home ownership by the elderly does appear to vary by community type. Ecosometrics (1981) reports home ownership for 90 percent of rural elderly farm families, 82 percent of nonmetropolitan household heads, and 56 percent of the urban elderly. This higher rate of home ownership means the rural elderly are more likely to be affected by problems of maintenance and repair and property tax increases.

In addition to being more likely to own their homes, the rural elderly are much more likely to live in single, detached dwelling units (approximately 86 percent compared to 54 percent for the metropolitan aged) (Bylund et al., 1980). This finding may reflect the desire of the rural elderly to live in such dwelling types, but it underscores the lack of adequate alternatives (e.g., apartments, group living quarters, subsidized housing). This high rate of single dwelling unit occupancy further increases the likelihood that the rural elderly will face housing repair and upkeep costs. As will be discussed later in this chapter, both the home ownership and dwelling type characteristics of the rural elderly have straightforward implications for the types of housing services and programs needed but rarely found in rural places.

Elderly homeowners have also lived in their homes longer than the non-elderly (Soldo, 1980), and Bylund et al. (1980) report that length of residence is on average greater for the non-metropolitan versus metropolitan elderly. This finding is substantiated by a more recent study done by the author in western New York (Krout, 1984). This longer tenure for the elderly in general, and the rural elderly in particular, means that the housing of the elderly is older (Kart, 1981). Bylund et al. (1980) report that 48 percent of the elderly's housing was built prior to 1940 versus 35 percent for all dwellings. The percentage is even greater (60 percent) for the rural elderly (Atchley and Miller, 1975). This has several important implications. The homes of the elderly and especially the rural elderly are less well insulated. Being less modern, they tend to have more maintenance problems and deficiencies and are more likely to be functionally inadequate (Soldo, 1980). In addition, these older homes are worth less money (Soldo, 1980). Atchley and Miller (1975) argue that the homes of the rural elderly have lower values because of their age and more deteriorated condition.

HOUSING QUALITY

Perhaps no other aspect of elderly housing has been given more attention than has been given to that of housing quality. Housing quality implies the presence or absence of certain characteristics by which a dwelling can be evaluated or judged as to its adequacy and is generally determined by an examination of the physical characteristics of the structure itself (Bylund et al., 1979). Given the fact that the housing for the elderly is on average older, it is not surprising to find reports indicating the elderly are more likely to live in housing that lacks one or more of the characteristics seen as necessary for modern living. Soldo (1980), for example, reports that at least 30 percent of elderly live in substandard housing, while Carp (1975) notes that one-third of the elderly's housing lacks basic plumbing or a telephone, with an even greater proportion lacking central heating.

Housing problems appear to be particularly acute in rural areas. The New York State Senate (1980) reports that 46 percent of the 30 million Americans who live in overcrowded dwellings or houses with incomplete plumbing reside in nonmetropolitan areas and that one-half of the substandard housing units in the United States are in rural places. Rural America (1977) claims that the situation is even worse, with 60 percent of the nation's inadequate housing located in rural areas. And it is the rural elderly who are proportionally more likely to live in this inadequate housing.

Several sources report that at least one-quarter of the substandard housing located in rural areas is occupied by the elderly (Rural America, 1977; White House Conference on Aging, 1971). One comprehensive review of rural/urban differences argues that national data from both the census and annual housing surveys provide "overwhelming evidence that elderly individuals in rural areas reside in housing of much poorer quality than the urban elderly" (Ecosometrics, 1981, 101). For example, data from the annual housing survey show that the housing of the rural elderly is twice as likely to have housing deficiencies as that of the urban elderly. This is measured by two criteria: the lack or insufficiency of certain basic necessities (kitchen, plumbing, heating) and the presence of undesirable features such as broken steps or leaky roofs. Rural elderly renters are twice as likely as homeowners to have one or more deficiencies. Similar findings are reported by a number of other authors (Bylund et al., 1980; Noll, 1978; Struyk, 1977).

For example, Ecosometrics (1981) reports that data from annual housing surveys in the late 1970's indicate that 12 percent of rural elderly households had one or more housing deficiencies, while Bylund et al. (1980) report that 2 percent of the elderly-owner–occupied dwellings in metropolitan areas lacked complete plumbing but that the comparable figure for nonmetropolitan areas was 8 percent. Rural America (1977) reports that the rural elderly fare even worse in comparison to the urban elderly. They found that 21 percent of the homes of nonmetropolitan elderly lacked all or some plumbing, while the same condition existed for only 4 percent of the metropolitan elderly.

Perhaps one of the most thorough rural/urban comparisons of the elderly's housing quality was conducted by Bylund et al. (1979). They note that most studies of housing quality are inadequate because they are based on census data on individual items (plumbing, heat, age) and thus give too narrow a view of quality and probably underestimate the number of substandard units. Those studies that do use summation procedures pay little attention to the reliability or validity of the resulting index. Bylund et al. (1979) used data from the 1975 national annual housing survey to develop a housing quality index for almost 12,000 elderly-headed households. The index was based on 22 deficiency items that yielded two groups: a facility index that measured the existence of basic housing items such as plumbing, telephones, and running water, and a condition index measuring problems with the structure such as leaky roofs or broken plaster or steps. Each dwelling unit was then assigned a score for each index (Bylund et al., 1979).

The size and representativeness of the sample allowed an

analysis of these scores based on a six-point size-of-place-continuum that ranged from rural farm to metropolitan central city. The authors conclude that, in general, the larger the size of place, the better the quality of housing for both the facility and condition index. For example, 68 percent of the farm dwellings and 88 percent of the metropolitan units had complete facilities. On the other hand, 20 percent of the farm versus 4 percent of the metropolitan elderly facilities lacked two or more facilities. In terms of conditions, 29 percent of the farm versus 66 percent of the metropolitan dwellings had no problems.

Researchers carrying out case studies of the rural elderly in specific geographic areas have found considerable housing problems as well. Larson and Youmans (1978) report that one-half of a sample of Kentucky rural elderly stated their housing needed repairs, while 14 percent of the dwellings did not have telephones. Montgomery et al. (1980) report that the housing of a sample of rural elderly in the South had many defects. These studies underscore the fact that research such as that done by Bylund et al. (1979) is based on national data on the rural elderly in general and that significant housing quality differences exist between geographic regions and between population subgroups (Atchley and Miller, 1975; Montgomery et al., 1980).

It would appear that a number of factors contribute to the observed rural elderly housing disadvantage. The supposed lower income and education levels of the rural elderly could well play a role. Yet Bylund (1981) reports that objective housing quality differences based on residence remain when rural/urban income and education differences are taken into account. However, other explanations abound. As will be discussed shortly, few housing programs are made available in rural areas (Kim, 1981), and the programs that are available are often inappropriate given the housing circumstances and needs of the rural elderly (New York State Senate, 1980). Finally, Bylund (1985) notes that substandard rural elderly housing units are often not seen by others by virtue of their location in isolated or sparsely populated areas and that the rural elderly are reluctant and even resistant to seeking governmental assistance in dealing with housing problems.

HOUSING SATISFACTION

Given the preceding discussion of housing, one would expect the elderly in general, and the rural elderly in particular, to express a significant degree of dissatisfaction with their housing. However, as in the case of self-assessed physical health, research has shown that although housing problems may exist for a significant percentage of the elderly in an objective sense, they themselves appear to be quite satisfied with their housing environments. A 1974 National Council on the Aging/Harris survey found that only 4 percent of the elderly identified housing as a real problem (Harris, 1978). Some authors have suggested the elderly are just as satisfied with their housing as other population groups (Weeks, 1984), while others (Kart, 1981) state the elderly's assessment of their dwelling units is somewhat more positive than the non-elderly's. Kart (1981) notes this is due to the stronger attachment the elderly feel to their homes because they are more likely to be homeowners (financial investment) and have lived there longer or because of the lack of other housing options (psychological defense). This satisfaction may also reflect a cohort effect in that the elderly grew up in less modern housing and thus are satisfied with less, or it may reflect an aging effect in that housing quality expectations lower with age to reduce the gap between expectations and reality (Montgomery et al., 1980).

Since the rural elderly are more likely to be homeowners and to have lived in their houses longer, one would expect them to be at least as satisfied with their housing as the elderly in general. The existing literature supports this expectation (Atchley and Miller, 1975; Montgomery et al., 1980). Montgomery et al. (1980) report 95 percent of a sample of elderly from the rural South felt their housing fully met their needs.

HOUSING PROGRAMS

The major thrust in federally sponsored housing programs that has most affected the elderly has been the construction of subsidized housing projects (Regnier, 1983). By 1978, the elderly occupied almost one-half of all low income subsidized housing, but most of this was not specifically designed for older people (Weeks, 1984). The overwhelming consensus of almost all who have given attention to the matter is that federal and many state programs have been largely geared to cities and that the housing problems in rural areas have virtually been ignored by existing policies and programs.

For example, Carp (1975) notes that only 2 percent of the combined efforts of the Department of Housing and Urban Development and Farmers Home Administration have been directed to deal with substandard rural housing. And the Farmers Home Administration itself (1980) estimates that only one-sixth of the nation's housing resources were allocated to nonmetropolitan areas in the mid 1970's. Not surprisingly, federal and state initiatives have had little impact on the housing problems of the rural elderly (Bylund et al., 1979). Atchley and Miller (1975) voice a similar sentiment and note further that much of the aid that does get to rural areas goes for multi-unit housing and not to those who reside in single family dwelling units. In addition, existing programs are developed from an urban perspective and are not appropriate for rural areas or populations (New York State Senate, 1980). Thus, a significant gap exists between housing programs and the needs of the rural elderly.

The National Rural Strategy Conference (1979) notes that not only do rural areas receive a disproportionately small percentage of housing funds, but they also do not have the personnel or expertise at the local level to adequately deal with housing issues. Thus, in addition to calling for more funding for rural elderly housing programs, the National Rural Strategy Conference (1979) has identified the following as necessary for a comprehensive response to the housing problems of the rural elderly:

• the development of a national housing policy with a long-range plan for the rural elderly

• the coordination by the Administration on Aging of all federal housing programs for the rural elderly

• an increase in Farmers Home Administration grants for home repair and rehabilitation and outreach programs for the low income elderly

• greater flexibility in state and federal housing codes and regulations

• an increase in weatherization and rehabilitation of low income houses

- a document to be produced by the Administration on Aging that clearly explains the federal housing programs available to the rural elderly
- a wide range of research and development projects on the feasibility, adequacy, and cost of alternative living arrangements

TRANSPORTATION

As was noted in the chapter introduction, transportation is seen as an important factor in the lives of the elderly. Elderly who lack access to appropriate and affordable transportation may experience restricted participation in social and recreational activities as well as restricted access to important services and reduced life satisfaction or morale.

TRANSPORTATION AVAILABILITY

When thinking about transportation and mobility in the United States, the privately owned automobile most often comes to mind. In fact, the White House Council on Aging (1981) reports that this mode of transportation accounts for 80 percent of all personal trips. It was noted earlier that the elderly are less likely to own cars. What about rural/urban differences in this area? One might be surprised to learn that a number of researchers have reported the rural elderly to have higher rates of car ownership than the urban elderly (Cottrell, 1975; McGhee, 1983). A study of western New York elderly recently completed by the author (Krout, 1984) found that 92 percent of the elderly living in nonmetropolitan communities of less than 2,500 and 64 percent of their central city counterparts reported owning a car. However, one must be careful to generalize this high rate of car ownership to the elderly nationally. Ecosometrics (1981), for example, reports that 45 percent of the rural elderly do not own cars.

It is an understatement to say that most rural communities are not well-served by taxis, inter-city buses, or other public transportation modes (McKelvey, 1979). The National Rural Strategy Conference (1979) presents some startling data on public transportation in rural areas. Only 284 of the 20,000 areas with populations of 50,000 or less have public transit systems, and as few as 11 percent of communities of less than 2,500 have inter-city bus service. Thus, what appears to be an advantage to the rural elderly is in fact evidence of an important disadvantage. The greater rate of car ownership among the rural elderly is attributed almost wholly to the lack of alternative modes of travel (public or commercial) (Cottrell, 1975; Ecosometrics, 1981; Lassey et al., 1980; McGhee, 1983).

As a result, the rural elderly are forced into a greater reliance on the automobile (which they may not have or which may be too expensive to run) because of the paucity of public transportation in rural areas (Cottrell, 1975). The low density of population in these more sparsely populated areas makes the cost of public transportation generally prohibitive. The net result is that the rural elderly may find themselves isolated and often unable to utilize essential and valuable social services (Harris, 1978; Nelson, 1980). A report by the New York State Senate (1980) estimates that less than one percent of the rural elderly working outside the home have access to public transportation.

Thus, while the rural elderly are more likely to own their own vehicle, public transportation is essentially not available. The author (Krout, 1984) has found the urban elderly four times more likely than the rural elderly to use other modes of transportation than a car. It would appear that the rural elderly are particularly vulnerable to transportation problems because they are so dependent on private car ownership—there is no alternative. Thus, the rural elderly who are too poor to own a car, too unhealthy to drive, or simply do not want to drive may find themselves isolated. Orr (1978), for example, reports that rural elderly females are twice as likely not to drive a car as males. Since the distances to necessary goods and services are greater in rural areas, walking may be out of the question (Kim, 1981), and even those elderly who live in small communities have limited choices for shopping and may have to pay higher prices for goods and services. These longer distances may also create greater problems for the rural elderly in terms of maintaining informal networks for social and recreational purposes and traveling to jobs or volunteer activities (New York State Senate, 1980).

TRANSPORTATION ADEQUACY

A fundamental question is the degree to which the rural elderly experience transportation difficulties and the effect that this restriction of mobility has on their daily lives. Most of the existing research on transportation and the elderly has been carried out on urban places (Gombeski and Smolensky, 1980). National statistics are not available to answer these questions, and the findings from local studies are not consistent. For example, Gunter (1980) reports that 7 percent of a rural Illinois sample saw lack of transportation as a problem, while Gombeski and Smolensky (1980) report that 6 percent of a rural Texas elderly sample had been unable to see a doctor when necessary because of transportation problems. On the other hand, Schulte et al. (1978) found that 22 percent of a nonmetropolitan sample of Kentucky residents aged 60 and over reported transportation-related problems, and Kivett and Scott (1979) found that 38 percent of a North Carolina sample reported a problem with transportation. McGhee (1983) notes that the great diversity of population characteristics in different rural areas may account for these differences and that these characteristics may be more important than rurality in explaining transportation adequacy.

Few studies have used research designs to allow an examination of rural/urban differences on the elderly's perception of transportation adequacy. One study of the elderly residing in a nonmetropolitan county conducted by the author (Krout and Larson, 1980) found 11 percent of the respondents indicating that problems with transportation kept them from doing things. Although size-of-place differences were small, the elderly living in the open country were least likely to indicate these problems. A more recent study by the author (Krout, 1984) of the metropolitan versus nonmetropolitan elderly in western New York found no significant differences based on residence for transportation problems.

Who among the rural elderly are most likely to report transportation problems? It is not surprising to find that the more disadvantaged among the rural elderly (those with limited economic, physical, and social resources) report greater transportation difficulties. (Kivett and Scott, 1979; McGhee, 1983). Several studies report that women and widows are particularly susceptible to such problems (Cottrell, 1971; Patton, 1975). This is partly because women are much less likely to own a car (Special Committee on Aging, 1982). Patton (1975) found that only 8 percent of elderly males but two-thirds of elderly females did not have access to an automobile. This appears to largely account for Cutler's (1975) finding that whereas older and younger rural males did not differ significantly on mobility (trips), older females were a lot less mobile than younger females.

It is clear that not all those rural elderly who are without automobiles experience problems with transportation: some are provided with transportation by friends and relatives. Powers et al. (1975) note that inter-generational support is frequently extended to the rural elderly. For example, Gombeski and Smolensky (1980) found that 17 percent of a small rural Texas elderly sample rode to the doctor with relatives and 9 percent rode with friends. Larson and Youmans (1978) also found that friends or relatives were most often relied upon for transportation assistance. One of the most recent studies of transportation and the rural elderly (McGhee, 1983) found that 43 percent of a rural Indiana elderly sample could be classified as transportation-dependent (they did not drive themselves or generally walk places). Sex was the most important predictor of transportation dependency, followed by variables such as vehicle ownership, purpose of trip, marital status, physical mobility, satisfaction with neighborhood, and education. Transportation dependents were more likely to be female, non–car-owners, unmarried, less physically mobile, more satisfied with neighbors, and less well educated.

Unfortunately, very little research had been conducted on the impact of transportation inadequacy on the rural elderly. It would seem obvious that those rural elderly who do not have their own means of transportation would be limited in terms of their participation in the community and might suffer declines in physical and/or mental health. Kivett (1979), for example, reports that a problem with transportation was the most important factor in discriminating between those rural North Carolina elderly who did report loneliness and those who did not.

TRANSPORTATION PROGRAMS

A number of public programs exist that provide transportation services for the elderly. A New York State Senate report (1980) notes that eight federal agencies administer 31 such programs, and the White House Conference on Aging (1981) reported that in 1979, some 3,000 transportation projects for the elderly were fully or partially supported by Older Americans Act funds. However, very few of these are aimed at the rural elderly. This probably reflects the strong big-city bias of U.S. transportation programs in general.

Kim (1981) notes that there is no federal agency for rural transportation comparable to the Urban Mass Transportation Administration (UMTA) and that a very small percentage of UMTA's funds go to rural areas. The National Rural Strategy Conference (1979) has argued that federal agencies such as UMTA and the Farmers Home Administration must work together to improve and administer transportation programs in rural areas. Further, it suggests that the Administration on Aging assemble a transit task force to address the rural elderly transportation situation and that federal and state legislation should mandate better coordination of rural transportation services. Rural areas simply do not have the dollars to support transportation programs without federal subsidies.

RESEARCH NEEDS

Both the housing and transportation of the rural aged constitute areas in need of considerably more attention from gerontologists. While there have been case studies on some aspects of these topics and national statistics are collected on others, some very important basic research questions have not been answered or in some cases even asked. For example, detailed statistics are collected by the Bureau of the Census through annual housing surveys on many aspects of the facilities and physical condition of dwelling units. An analysis of these statistics indicates that the condition of the rural elderly's housing is worse than that of the urban elderly. But what does this mean? First of all, these statistics are based on the reports of those who reside in the housing and thus may under- or over-report problems. Given that the rural elderly do not report being less satisfied with their housing, could they not be reporting fewer problems than objectively exist? Second, given the rural/urban comparability of elderly housing satisfaction, what do the objective differences indicate? Too little research has been done on housing perception and satisfaction of the rural elderly.

Given the greater potential for isolation of the rural elderly due to the sparser population and almost non-existent public transportation of rural areas, the question of how the housing of the rural elderly impacts on their daily activities and health and social status becomes of even greater importance. Such information is basic to the design and implementation of programs aimed at dealing with these problems. Yet there is very little systematic research on this question or on how rurality interacts with other factors such as race, sex, and income to affect housing impacts.

In addition, it has been noted that housing programs have largely bypassed rural areas and the rural elderly. However, little is known of the rural elderly's awareness of such programs or how they perceive them. Knowledge of this issue is important for another policy question—the alternatives to existing housing arrangements for the rural elderly. If housing problems do significantly affect the rural elderly, the logical follow-up question is how those problems can most appropriately (given the economic characteristics, values, etc., of rural populations) and effectively be addressed. Are subsidized apartments or congregate housing units the answer? If so, how (if at all) should urban models of these programs be adapted to rural environments?

The same questions of impact have also not been investigated in regard to transportation. Public transportation is rare indeed in rural areas and the elderly who do not drive have few alternatives beyond relatives, friends, and neighbors. But how are the rural elderly affected by this transportation situation? What are the costs (economical, physical, and psychological) of these transportation patterns, and what are the benefits, if any? When transportation problems exist for the rural elderly, how can they be most effectively and appropriately overcome?

A fundamental issue is whether or not the rural elderly have access to, or must bear a transportation burden in using, social and health services. If problems of access or burden exist, how can they best be remedied? Should the services be brought to the elderly (e.g., mobile units), or should the people be brought to the services (e.g., through the use of vans and volunteer drivers)? Such programs do exist, but a sufficient research base has not been built to allow reasoned assessments of their effectiveness or the program and policy alternatives in these areas.

SUMMARY

This chapter has attempted to provide an overview of the housing and transportation situation of the rural elderly and of the problems in these areas that are particular to rural places. It has been observed that the rural elderly are more likely than the urban elderly to be homeowners, but their homes are older, less valuable, evidence a greater lack of basic facilities, and are more likely to have housing deficiencies. Yet, the rural elderly report comparable levels of housing satisfaction. The reasons for these housing attitudes and the impact of housing deficiencies on the rural elderly have not been adequately researched.

In terms of transportation, the rural elderly are much more likely to own a private vehicle, largely because of the lack of commercial or public transportation alternatives in rural areas. Although national statistics are not available, a number of studies show that the rural elderly see transportation as a major problem for them. And while gerontological research indicates that appropriate and adequate transportation is an important correlate of life satisfaction and social participation among the elderly in general, the impact of transportation problems on the status of the rural elderly has not been sufficiently examined. Important questions concerning the role of transportation in comparison to other factors have also not been addressed.

Finally, the literature suggests that the public response to both the housing and transportation needs of the rural elderly has been totally inadequate. Few federal resources have been allocated to deal with these issues in rural areas, and local responses are hindered by lack of money and expertise. It would appear that greater coordination and guidance is needed in the mish-mash of programs that do or could affect transportation and housing problems. Existing programs have arisen in a piecemeal fashion and do not meet needs. Equally important, the research necessary to inform policy makers on decisions as to what programs are needed and how they would be best structured has not been carried out.

While all the topics covered in this book are important, certainly none are more important than housing and transportation. The home environment is so crucial to the elderly because it is where they spend so much time. The cost and condition of the housing unit is central to how well the elderly are able to manage independent living in the community. Transportation, on the other hand, reinforces the adequacy of that housing by providing a link to all those basic goods and services necessary for survival. The gaps in the knowledge of these two areas have significant ramifications for the understanding of the rural elderly and the ability of society to meet their needs.

REFERENCES

Atchley, R.C., and S.J. Miller. 1975, "Housing and the Rural Aged," in *Rural Environments and Aging*, R.C. Atchley and T.O. Byerts (eds.), Gerontological Society, Washington, D.C.

Berghorn, F.J., et al. 1978, *The Urban Elderly: A Study of Life Satisfaction*, Allanheld, Osmun and Company Publishers, Montclair, New Jersey.

Bylund, R. 1981, "Housing Quality of the Elderly: The Importance of Size of Place of Residence," paper presented at the annual meeting of the Rural Sociological Society, Guelph, Ontario.

———. 1985, "Rural Housing Perspectives for the Aged," in *The Elderly in Rural Society*, R. Coward and G. Lee (eds.), Springer, New York.

Bylund, R.A., N.L. LeRay, and C.O. Crawford. 1979, "Housing Quality of the Elderly: A Rural-Urban Comparison," *Journal of Minority Aging*, 4, 14–24.

———. 1980, *Older American Households and Their Housing in 1975: A Metro-Nonmetro Comparison*, Agricultural Experiment Station, University Park, Pennsylvania.

Carp, F.M. 1975, "The Impact of Improved Housing on Morale and Life Satisfaction," *The Gerontologist*, 15, 515.

————. 1979, "Improving the Functional Quality of Housing and Environments for the Elderly Through Transportation," in *Environmental Context of Aging*, T.O. Byerts, S.C. Howell, and L.A. Pastalan (eds.), Garland Publishing, New York.

Cottrell F. 1971, "Transportation of the Older People in a Rural Community," *Sociological Focus*, 5, 29–40.

————. 1975, "Transportation of the Rural Aged," in *Rural Environments and Aging*, R.C. Atchley and T.O. Byerts (eds.), Gerontological Society, Washington, D.C.

Cutler, S.J. 1975, "Transportation and Change in Life Satisfaction," *The Gerontologist*, 15, 155–159.

Ecosometrics. 1981, *Review of Reported Differences Between the Rural and Urban Elderly: Status, Needs, Services, and Service Costs*, Final Report to the Administration on Aging (Contract No. 105–80–C–065), Washington, D.C.

Fengler, A.P., and N. Danigelis. 1982, "Residence, the Elderly Widow, and Life Satisfaction," *Research on Aging*, 4, 113–135.

Gombeski, W.R., and M.S. Smolensky. 1980, "Non-Emergency Health Transportation Needs of the Rural Texas Elderly," *The Gerontologist*, 20, 452–456.

Gunter, P.L. 1980, "A Survey of the Needs of the Rural Elderly in Selected Counties in Southern Illinois," Ph.d. diss., Southern Illinois University, Carbondale, Illinois.

Harris, C. 1978, *Fact Book on Aging: A Profile of America's Older Population*, National Council on the Aging, Washington, D.C.

Kart, C.S. 1981, *The Realities of Aging*, Allyn and Bacon, Boston.

Kaye, I. 1978, "The Brass Ring in the Golden Years," *Perspective on Aging*, January/February, 30–32.

Kim, P.K. 1981, "The Low Income Rural Elderly: Under-Served Victims of Public Inequity," in *Toward the Mental Health of the Rural Elderly*, P.K. Kim and C. Wilson (eds.), University Press of America, Washington, D.C.

Kivett, V.R., 1979, "Discriminators of Loneliness Among the Rural Elderly: Implications for Intervention," *The Gerontologist*, 19, 108–115.

Kivett, V.R., and J.R. Scott. 1979, *The Rural By-Passed Elderly*, Technical Bulletin No. 260, North Carolina Agricultural Research Service, University of North Carolina at Greensboro, Greensboro, North Carolina.

Krout, J.A. 1984, *The Utilization of Formal and Informal Support of the Aged:*

Rural Versus Urban Differences, final report to the Andrus Foundation, American Association of Retired Persons, Fredonia, New York.

Krout, J.A., and D. Larson. 1980, "Self-Assessed Needs of the Rural Elderly," paper presented at the annual meeting of the Rural Sociological Society, Ithaca, New York.

Larson, D.K., and E.G. Youmans. 1978, *Problems of the Rural Elderly Households in Powell County, Kentucky*, U.S. Department of Agriculture, Washington, D.C.

Lassey, G., M. Lassey, and G. Lee. 1980, *Research and Public Service with the Rural Elderly: Proceedings of a Conference*, Western Rural Development Center, Oregon State University, Corvallis, Oregon.

McGhee, J.L. 1983, "Transportation Opportunity and the Rural Elderly: A Comparison of Objective and Subjective Indicators," *The Gerontologist*, 23, 505–511.

McKelvey, D.J. 1979, "Transportation Issues and Problems of the Rural Elderly," in *Location and Environment of the Elderly Population*, S.M. Golant (ed.), V.H. Winston and Sons, Washington, D.C.

Montgomery, J.E., A.C. Stubbs, and S.S. Day. 1980, "The Housing Environment of the Rural Elderly," *The Gerontologist*, 20, 444–451.

National Rural Strategy Conference. 1979, *Improving Services for the Rural Elderly*, National Strategy Conference on Improving Service Delivery to the Rural Elderly, Des Moines, Iowa.

Nelson, G. 1980, "Social Services to the Urban and Rural Aged: The Experience of Area Agencies on Aging," *The Gerontologist*, 20, 200–207.

New York State Senate. 1980, *Old Age and Ruralism: A Case of Double Jeopardy—Report on the Rural Elderly*, New York State Senate, Albany, New York.

Noll, P.F. 1978, *Federally Assisted Housing Programs for the Elderly in Rural Areas: Programs and Prospects*, Housing Assistance Council, Washington, D.C.

Orr, R.H. 1978, "The Need for Transportation Services Among Rural Elderly," *Tennessee Farm and Home Science*, January/February/March, 16–18.

Patton, C.V. 1975, "Age Groupings and Travel in a Rural Area," *Rural Sociology*, 40, 55–63.

Powers, E.A, P. Keith, and W.J. Goudy. 1975, "Family Relationships and Friendships," in *Rural Environments and Aging*, R.C. Atchley and T.O. Byerts (eds.), Gerontological Society, Washington, D.C.

Regnier, V. 1983, "Housing and Environment," in *Aging: Scientific Per-*

spectives and Social Issues, D.S. Woodruff and J.E. Berrin (eds.), Brooks/Cole, Monterey, California.

Rural America. 1977, *Rural America Factsheet: The Elderly*, Rural America, Washington, D.C.

Schulte, P., J.M. Brockway, and S.A. Murrell. 1978, *Kentucky Elderly Needs Assessment Survey*, Urban Studies Centers, University of Louisville, Louisville, Kentucky.

Soldo, B. 1980, "America's Elderly in the 1980's," *Population Bulletin*, 35, 15–18.

Special Committee on Aging. 1982, *Developments in Aging: 1981*, vol. 1, U.S. Senate, No. 97–364, U.S. Government Printing Office, Washington, D.C.

Struyk, R.J. 1977, "The Housing Situation of Elderly Americans," *The Gerontologist*, 17, 130–139.

Ward, R.A. 1984, *The Aging Experience: An Introduction to Social Gerontology*, Harper and Row, New York.

Weeks, J.R. 1984, *Aging*, Wadsworth Publishing, Belmont, California.

White House Conference on Aging. 1971, *The Rural and the Poor Elderly*, U.S. Government Printing Office, Washington, D.C.

———. 1981, *Chartbook on Aging in America*, White House Conference on Aging, Washington, D.C.

8   INFORMAL SUPPORT: FAMILY, FRIENDS, AND NEIGHBORS

INTRODUCTION

There is a tendency in our society to see the elderly as characterized by social isolation, living alone with little or no contact with family or others. It is true that as people age, they are more likely to lose a spouse—14 percent of males and 51 percent of females over aged 65 were widowed in 1980 (U.S. Bureau of the Census, 1981). Nonetheless, the spouse is the primary support and confidant in later life (Shanas, 1979), and children frequently provide support, especially when an elderly parent loses a spouse. In fact, 80 percent of the elderly in the United States have at least one child, and there is extensive documentation to suggest that children provide for 70 to 80 percent of their elderly parent's emotional, health, and social needs (Brody, 1978; Cryns and Nowak, 1981; Shanas et al., 1968), with increasing amounts of such assistance provided as frailty increases (Cantor, 1975; Laurie, 1978).

And it is not just the relatives of the elderly who provide them with significant social contact and support. Friends and neighbors also play important roles in the lives of the elderly. Typically, the elderly rely on these sources occasionally for assistance with impersonal tasks such as yard work, shopping, or just socializing (Bultena, et al., 1971; Cantor, 1979; Kaplan and Fleisher, 1981). Friends and neighbors may be relied on more heavily by those elderly who are not married or do not have children. Taken together, the family, friends, and neighbors of the elderly are often referred to collectively as "informal networks of support."

This topic is particularly appropriate for the investigation at hand for several reasons. First, the past ten years have seen an explosion in attention paid to informal networks and the support they provide the elderly. Second, one of the more enduring images of rural America is that of the family, self-reliant and caring for its own—especially the elderly. The presumed strength of traditional values (particularly those of familial obligation, filial responsibility, and Christian duty) thought to characterize rural rather than urban populations has led to expectations of stronger, better integrated, and more extensive networks of familial support among the rural elderly (Deimling and Huber, 1981; Heller 1970, 1976; Lee, 1980).

And, it has also been suggested that the rural elderly are more likely to turn to informal networks because of the difficulty of utilizing, or the absence of, alternative formal services (Deimling and Huber, 1981). City living, by comparison, is seen as disruptive of kinship interaction and friendship patterns (Milgrim, 1970; Wirth, 1936). However, the out-migration of rural youth due to relatively recent secular trends toward higher education, independence, and upward mobility might be presumed to thwart this natural caregiving process in rural areas by both challenging the structure of traditional kin values and reducing the number of caregivers available to the elderly (Nowak, 1982).

The following chapter reviews the existing research to answer, as best as possible, the question of the availability and utilization of informal networks for the rural elderly and how these may differ from the patterns found for the elderly residing in more urbanized settings. Unfortunately, few studies have been carried out on rural family life or kinship patterns in general, and while it would be unwarranted to assume that no rural/urban differences exist in this area, the precise nature and correlates of these differences have not been identified.

MARITAL STATUS AND CHILDREN

As was noted in Chapter 2, the elderly living in nonmetropolitan areas are more likely to be married than the metropolitan elderly. For example, a national probability sample of the aged studied in the early 1970's found that 51 percent of the rural versus 43 percent of the urban elderly were married (Schooler, 1975). The rural advantage, especially among farm dwellers, is substantiated by 1980 census data as well. Thus, the nonmetropolitan aged are most likely to live with a spouse. An earlier study by Shanas et al. (1968) found the rural elderly more likely to be living with relatives, and census data show that less than 10 percent of the rural elderly live with children—essentially the same as the elderly as a whole (Powers, Keith, and Goudy, 1975).

One of the more commonly held beliefs about rural families is that they are considerably larger and have more children than urban families, and that the rural elderly should have a larger network of children and siblings to call on for assistance. However, several studies have not found this to be the case. Deimling and Huber (1981) report similar household sizes for elderly-headed households in a three-state sample, and the author's recent study of 600 elderly individuals in western New York found no significant differences based on residence in the number of children. However, the nonmetropolitan elderly were slightly less likely to have no children and slightly more likely to have three or four children (Krout, 1984).

It is not the absolute number of children, but the number of "readily available" children and other relatives, that gerontologists see as most important in providing support to the elderly. The term "readily available" usually refers to geographic closeness or residential proximity—a factor that researchers have found to be an important determinant of helping behavior (Adams, 1968; Bengston et al., 1976; Lee, 1980). Several researchers have reported that due to the out-migration of the young from rural areas, a smaller percentage of the rural elderly than of the urban elderly have their children living in their community. Bultena (1969) reports this for a sample from Wisconsin, and Bultena et al. (1971) for a sample in Iowa. Others have reported just the opposite (Shanas et al., 1968; Youmans, 1977). In fact, the recent study carried out by the author in western New York found community size unrelated to the potential for contact with children (measured by the number and proximity of children) (Krout, 1984).

Thus, the relationship between residence and proximity of

children has not clearly been established. The most supportable statement is that both rural and urban elders generally have at least one child living within a half hour of them. Kivett (1976) reports that 71 percent of a sample of elderly living in a North Carolina nonmetropolitan county with children had at least one child living in that county. A number of other researchers have found that approximately two-thirds of rural elderly parents in different parts of the country have at least one child living within a half-hour drive (Bultena, 1969; Shanas et al., 1968; Youmans, 1963). The question of proximity of the nearest child has important bearing on the issue of familial contact and the amount of assistance provided the elderly because, as noted, geographic distance is the most important determinant of kinship interaction (Lee, 1980).

CONTACT WITH CHILDREN

The results of studies examining rural/urban differences in the frequency of contact between elderly parents and their children are not consistent but do lend support to the statement that the urban elderly have somewhat more interaction than the rural elderly (Bultena, 1969; Krout, 1984; Youmans, 1963). Youmans's (1963) study of a sample of Kentucky aged reports this finding even though the urban parents lived on average farther away from their children than did their rural counterparts. This apparent paradox may be explained by the lower incomes of the rural sample and the greater difficulty of travel in rural areas. In fact, Youmans (1963) also found that the rural elderly were much less likely to visit their children but rather were more dependent on their children's coming to them, further suggesting that a lack of resources inhibited the rural elderly's interaction patterns. And as Lee and Cassidy (1985) note, Youmans's research was conducted in a region of the country where several other studies have shown very strong kinship ties. Yet, Youmans (1963) also found that proximity was positively associated with interaction for both his rural and urban samples.

Bultena's (1969) data come from a Wisconsin sample in which the urban elderly lived closer to their children and many of the rural elderly's children had left their parents' community. The

more recent study conducted by the author (Krout, 1984) revealed interaction patterns similar to those reported by Youmans
(1963) and Bultena (1969). Frequency of contact with children
was found to be positively related to community size in a multiple regression analysis. However, the role played by proximity
to children is not as easily interpreted as was the case for the
earlier studies.

The author's research collected data from the elderly living in
four different community types in western New York State: nonmetropolitan farm and rural (less than 2,500), nonmetropolitan
2,500 and up, metropolitan suburban, and metropolitan central
city. Fifty-eight percent of the nonmetropolitan farm and rural
elderly reported that their first-mentioned and usually oldest
child lived within 15 minutes, while the figure for the elderly
living in other communities ranged from 48 to 50 percent. For
the second child mentioned, the nonmetropolitan urban and
metropolitan suburban elderly were much more likely to report
a distance of under 15 minutes than either the nonmetropolitan
rural or central city elderly. Thus, the relationship between community size and distance in time to children was not linear or
uniform for different children. Further, a summed potential child-
contact score created with data combining the proximity and
number of children was not found to be significantly related to
community type in a multivariate analysis.

However, the results of these studies should not be interpreted as evidence that the rural elderly have low frequency of
contact with their children. Kivett and Scott (1979) report that
75 percent of the elderly in a North Carolina rural county with
children report a daily visit with at least one child. The author's
research found that 67 percent and 53 percent of the western
New York nonmetropolitan rural and urban elderly with a child
reported at least one contact a week with a child (Krout, 1984).

It should be noted that face-to-face interaction is not the only
form of elderly/child interaction that can play a part in the lives
of the aged. Other forms include telephone and mail. In fact,
interaction via the latter two modes may be more frequent than
the former. For example, Powers and Liston (1971) report that
a sample of rural Iowa elderly had one-third of their contact with
children via face-to-face interaction and one-half of their contact

via the telephone. When mail and telephone were added to face-to-face interaction, 94 percent had a minimum of one weekly child contact and 63 percent had two or more.

CONTACT WITH SIBLINGS

Gerontological research has clearly shown that relatives other than children, such as siblings, play relatively minor roles in providing assistance to the elderly (Cantor, 1979; Lopata, 1979). However, this does not mean that they are never important, and elderly with no children or children who live far away may rely considerably on other kin (Cummings and Schneider, 1966; Kivett, 1983). Other variables central to the strength of the sibling relationship are sex of siblings (Adams, 1968; Shanas et al., 1968); marital status (Shanas et al., 1968); ethnic background (Johnson, 1982); social class (Adams, 1968); and age (Cummings and Schneider, 1966).

Kivett's (1983) study of a sample of elderly in the rural Piedmont area of North Carolina found that older adults had an average of three siblings—the majority of which lived within half an hour's trip. However, only a small percentage of the respondents noted receiving assistance from them. Twenty-four percent had received transportation assistance, and 12 percent had gotten help during an illness. While the amount of help from siblings increased as the health and number of children of the elder decreased and proximity increased, Kivett concludes that siblings were of little functional importance in terms of services provided, while their psychological importance may have been of greater significance. This relatively small amount of interaction between rural elderly and siblings was also noted in an Iowa study by Powers et al. (1981).

NATURE OF SUPPORT

The gerontological literature suggests that who an elderly person turns to for assistance depends on the nature of that assistance. For serious needs or emotional support, the elderly rely primarily on children, and those without children turn next to relatives or friends (Lopata, 1973; Rosow, 1967; Shanas et al., 1968). This generalization would appear to apply regardless of residence. However, the bulk of assistance received by the rural elderly is in nonpersonal areas such as housework, shopping, and transportation and not in more personal areas such as getting dressed, getting in and out of bed, or bathing (Bultena et al., 1971; Goodfellow, 1983; Krout, 1984; Rosencranz et al., 1968).

It should be noted that the provision of assistance or support in specific tasks not only helps the elderly with those tasks but has additional benefits as well. For example, Dean and Lin (1977) report that close personal relationships between elderly and family members (and friends) are related to lower levels of stress and illness among the elderly. House (1981) argues further that familial support may act as a buffer between stress and health, reducing both the likelihood that a problem will arise and its impact. Besides these direct and indirect impacts of support on the elderly's health, informal network interaction has been found to be positively related to morale and life satisfaction (Rosow, 1967).

Although obviously important for familial contact and both emergency intervention and long-term assistance, the mere presence of and interaction with family members does not assure that care for either rural or urban elderly is available when needed. There is substantial literature on familial support in general to suggest that both sex and relationship of kin are more predictive of caregiving in later life than mere availability (Nowak, 1982). Daughters, daughters-in-law, and nieces follow spouses in order of their likelihood to assume primary caregiver roles. While little attention has been paid to rural/urban differences in this respect, there is a bit of evidence to suggest similarities between the two in *sex* of likely caregiver (i.e., female) but differences in *relationship* (i.e., in-laws are more likely to assume rural responsibilities, while nieces do so more among the urban) (Deimling and Huber, 1981).

It has been observed that contrary to popular stereotypes, the rural elderly have somewhat less frequent contact with their children than the urban elderly, though the contact for both is considerable. However, the quantity of contact itself does not speak to the nature of the interaction or the role children play in providing assistance to elderly parents. There is an important qualitative difference between visiting with someone and providing help in doing chores or carrying out personal activities such as bathing, dressing, etc. Once again, the image is that the rural elderly would be more likely to receive such assistance from children because it is often assumed that more nucleated forms of family relations result from urbanization and urban living and lead to a decline in the sense of obligation and support (or filial responsibility) young adults feel toward their elderly parents (Sauer et al., 1980).

Some research supports this position (Dinkel, 1984), while other studies have found the opposite or no rural/urban differences on attitudes toward filial responsibility. For example, Sauer et al. (1980) report that metropolitan adults were significantly more likely to endorse norms of filial responsibility than nonmetropolitan adults, while Wade and Sporakowski (1972) found no differences in these attitudes based on residence for an Illinois sample. One study conducted in a small Pennsylvania town found that adults did not think it was appropriate for the elderly to request assistance from their children—except in emergencies (Britton et al., 1961). And what of the rural elderly's expectations of their children? A study carried out in rural Iowa found that 80 percent of older men felt the family should help with health problems but only about one-half felt the same in the case of financial problems (Powers, Keith, and Goudy, 1981).

The data on actual assistance patterns of the rural elderly's children are somewhat contradictory. One national study (Shanas et al., 1968) and a study of small Missouri towns (Rosencranz et al., 1968) found that 60 percent of the rural elderly received some form of help from children. The elderly in a more recent study of two small Pennsylvania towns (Goodfellow, 1983) reported that 65 percent of the assistance they received came from family members. However, only 40 percent of the rural elderly samples in Iowa (Bultena et al., 1971) and Pennsylvania (Montgomery, 1965) reported receiving regular support from any source of help—children included.

CONTACT AND ASSISTANCE FROM FRIENDS AND NEIGHBORS

Friends and neighbors are also important components in the informal support networks of the elderly. Even though the use of friends and neighbors in the satisfaction of later life needs is typically restricted to "now and then" impersonal chores (Bultena, 1971; Kaplan and Fleisher, 1981) or emergency intervention in times of illness or disaster (Cantor, 1979; Kaplan and Fleisher, 1981), they should not be overlooked. Some of the functions they perform include acting as role models and providing support for important status changes such as widowhood and retirement (Lopata, 1978), serving as confidants (Pastorello, 1974), and expanding social networks (Rosow, 1967; Shanas et al., 1968). In addition, research has shown that number of friends is related to life satisfaction and feelings of loneliness and uselessness (Arling, 1976). The roles of friends and neighbors may differ. Ward (1978) notes that neighbors are in a better position to give immediate assistance and check on the well-being of the elderly.

Numerous studies of the rural elderly in different areas of the country would seem to indicate moderate to high levels of contact with friends and neighbors. For example, the rural elderly in Missouri (Rosencranz et al., 1968) and northern states (Britton and Britton, 1972) reported averages of six "close" friends and ten or more friends respectively. One-quarter of the Missouri sample stated they had 14 or more close friends. As for contact, Kivett (1976) and Kivett and Scott (1979) found that 60 and 71 percent of North Carolina rural elderly samples had either frequent (at least once a week) or occasional (at least once a month) contact with friends and neighbors. Scott (1981) found 56 percent of a rural Texas elderly sample had frequent, and 26 percent had occasional, visiting with friends or neighbors, and McKain (1967) found frequent or occasional visiting for 60 percent of a sample of older rural Kentuckians.

Not only do the rural elderly evidence a considerable amount of contact with friends and neighbors, but they also generally appear to be satisfied with this level. Several studies have reported that samples of rural elderly feel no need to make new friends (Berardo, 1967; Pihlblad and McNamara, 1965), and two-thirds of a rural North Carolina sample said they saw their friends and family as often as they would like (Kivett and Scott, 1979). The rural elderly appear to rely on friends and neighbors for the same type of assistance as the elderly in general. Goodfellow (1983) found that a sample of rural Pennsylvania elderly largely asked friends and neighbors for help with transportation and that friends and neighbors provided 13 percent of the support received by her respondents. Bultena et al. (1971) report friends providing assistance to a sample of Iowa elderly in impersonal areas such as yard work and shopping.

The demographics of rural areas can be seen to alternatively facilitate and inhibit interaction between the elderly and their friends and neighbors. Recall that small towns have higher percentages of elderly, thus affording greater availability of age peers. At the same time, the low density and limited public and other transportation resources may result in greater social isolation. Other factors also affect the extent of friendship networks and neighborly assistance among the rural elderly. Powers et al. (1975) observe that the extent of friendship networks varies directly with length of residence in the area and stability of the neighborhood and its social homogeneity, and indirectly with the length of time assistance is given. That is, as needs become chronic, assistance from friends and neighbors is deferred to familial or professional givers of care (Cantor, 1979). Findings on the urban aged showing friendship and neighboring patterns related to social class factors such as income, race, and occupation may also apply to the rural elderly (Rosenburg, 1976).

Unfortunately, relatively little systematic research has been carried out on rural/urban differences in the friend and neighbor interaction patterns of the elderly. The majority of existing studies do tend to support the conclusion that levels of such informal interaction are higher for rural older adults (Kivett, 1985; Mercier and Powers, 1984). For example, McKain (1967) found that the rural aged in Kentucky were more likely to know people within their communities, engaged in more informal visiting, and identified a larger number of persons as close friends. Schooler's (1975) analysis of data from a national sample found greater contact between the rural as opposed to urban elderly and their neighbors. The greater level of interaction found for the rural elderly may reflect the high concentrations and ethnic homogeneity of rural communities (Kivett, 1985).

RESEARCH NEEDS

Researchers have examined various aspects of informal network extensiveness, availability, contact, and support for the rural elderly. However, the existing studies provide only the most basic information, and it is clear that considerably more research must be carried out to shed light on the sometimes contradictory findings and to further the adequate understanding of the nature and consequences of interaction between the rural elderly and their family, friends, and neighbors. More precise research questions must be framed and appropriate methodologies adopted to determine if and how rural/urban differences in demography, social organization, and values affect informal network interaction patterns.

Kivett (1985) has identified five basic areas of needed research on this topic. First, she echoes the familiar call for more information on the rural elderly's interaction with kin and nonkin as well. The vast majority of research on the what, when, and how of such interaction and assistance has been carried out on urban populations. Second, she cites a need for more attention to the factors associated with such interaction. The role of traditional variables such as age, sex, class, etc., and how they are affected by rural versus urban residence has certainly been largely ignored. Third, she calls for more research on the quality of these interactions. As is true of most gerontological survey research, existing studies of the rural elderly and their informal networks focus heavily on the quantity of contact.

These three concerns all relate to the limitations and inadequacies of what gerontologists know about the informal network interaction and support of the rural elderly. Other scholars have noted similar concerns. For example, Nowak (1982) argues that little work has been done on community size variations in informal support in terms of the type of support, ranging from casual assistance with yard work or shopping to the intensive support given to the physically and/or mentally frail elderly. In addition, Nowak (1982) notes that too little attention has been paid to the different contexts in which support is given (that is, in the care receiver's or caregiver's residence) or to the organization, delivery, or efficiency of this type of care. With regard to rural/urban differences on these issues, knowledge about kin proximity and contact would be pertinent, particularly in rural areas, where distances between households tend to be greater. Nowak (1982) notes the importance of focusing on both the giver and the receiver of care as an interactional unit and argues that the tendency to focus on one or the other provides only part of the picture.

Kivett (1985) also bemoans the relative lack of emphasis on the impact of informal network interaction on the rural elderly. Many important questions remain concerning the benefits and possible detriments of informal support assistance. The fifth concern of Kivett (1985) involves the methodological shortcomings of existing research. She calls for more longitudinal and multivariate studies that identify both the direct and indirect effects of demographic and social factors on rural familial and non-kin interaction patterns. Other authors have sounded similar concerns. Powers et al. (1981) argue that many more comparative, longitudinal, and inter-regional studies of rural elderly family and non-kin networks must be carried out to overcome the limited data currently available. Further, they note that the existing research on the rural elderly and rural/urban differences in this area suffers from a regional bias, as many of the studies have been conducted in a small number of midwestern states (Iowa, Kentucky, Missouri, and Wisconsin).

Finally, Kivett (1985) calls attention to the importance of tracking how the dynamic nature of rural areas affects the role informal networks play in the lives of the rural elderly. It was noted early on in this book that during the 1970's, rural areas experienced a faster rate of population growth than metropolitan areas, with a reversal of net migration from out to in. This fact underscores the need to frame and carry out research on whether and how these demographic trends, by changing age structures or social networks, have decreased or increased opportunities for friendships or other forms of kin and nonkin social interaction. Kivett (1985) also asserts that research should be focused on the impacts of the in-migration of formerly urban elderly dwellers to rural areas. To the degree that new in-migrants differ in terms of socio-economic and ethnic characteristics or values, conflict may arise with the indigenous rural elderly population, or rural/urban differences in certain aspects of informal interaction may, in fact, be reduced.

A number of policy issues are suggested by the topic at hand. For example, it has been noted that the familial networks and contact of the rural elderly do not appear, at least on the basis of existing research, to differ much from those of the urban elderly. Given that the rural elderly are worse off in some areas and no better off in others than the urban elderly, there would appear to be a greater need for formal types of assistance. But as has been seen and will be discussed in considerably more detail in the next chapter, the availability, accessibility, and scope of such services in rural areas is often lacking. Thus, the stereotype of the rural older person receiving much more assistance from family and friends than the urban older person is not accurate. How then can this gap between need and informal and formal supports best be addressed? It would seem logical to assert that the same lack of resources that affects the rural elderly affects their informal supports as well. So the questions arise as to the degree to which these supports are willing and able to provide support and how good of a job they do.

A number of gerontologists have argued that many questions need to be answered regarding the appropriateness and effectiveness of expecting too much from informal support networks. Biegel and Maguire (1982) have argued that informal care of the elderly is not a cure-all, may duplicate services available from formal agencies, and can even undo the positive aspects of professional help. Coward (1981) also has identified a number of potential negative effects on elderly care recipients, including perpetuation of misinformation (especially in regard to health) and the avoidance of seeking needed professional assistance. He also notes that caregivers may suffer from physical, financial, and emotional strain and that internal network dynamics may be upset due to the intrusion of representatives of formal organizations. The need to examine these questions as they relate to the rural elderly is particularly pressing.

SUMMARY

This chapter has discussed the familial and nonfamilial informal networks of the rural elderly. A topic of considerable interest to gerontologists in the last several decades, the issue of informal support is of particular importance to the analysis of the rural elderly because of the stereotypic view of rural families as being so strong and supportive of their kin and the notion that everyone is a good neighbor in rural areas. While existing studies of the rural elderly's informal support networks cannot be said to be definitive, they do present a picture by and large not significantly different from that found for the elderly in general. Some rural/urban variations do appear to exist. The rural elderly are more likely to be living with a spouse, and some research suggests that the children of the urban elderly live closer to and have more contact with their elderly parents than is true for rural areas. Other research suggests that the rural elderly have more contact with friends and neighbors. Overall, however, it would appear appropriate to conclude that the existing research does not support the stereotype of the super-supportive rural informal network or the picture of the isolated rural elderly. The rural elderly would appear to have interaction and support patterns with children, other kin, and friends and neighbors not widely different from the elderly who reside in other places.

It is clear, however, that much more research needs to be carried out on the informal support networks of the rural elderly. Many of the existing studies have involved fairly small samples in the Midwest, and few attempts have been made to replicate findings. Rather, the research is made up largely of descriptive studies that have not built on previous work and moved ahead to delineate and examine new substantive topics. A number of fundamental questions concerning the nature and impact of informal support from various sources have not been addressed for the rural elderly in general, in terms of rural/urban differences or in regard to rural elderly subgroups (class, ethnicity, sex, etc.).

Such basic information is very important for the consideration of the policy implications of informal support research. For example, it appears that the rural elderly receive considerable but not unusual assistance from these supports. However, this by no means indicates that these informal networks are doing the job without considerable burden or that they could handle more tasks. The question remains as to how public resources can best be integrated to both support and complement these efforts. Further, the observed lack of large rural/urban differences in informal support should not lead one to conclude that policy and program formulation need pay no attention to rural informal support or that rural areas can be ignored while resources continue to be provided to urban populations (Lee and Cassidy, 1985). In fact, as Lee and Cassidy (1985) point out, if their kin networks were as strong as legend would have it, the rural elderly would have *less* need for formal services, but this is not the case.

In conclusion, the question of the nature and impact of familial and nonfamilial networks is central to an understanding of the rural elderly and is one that needs considerably more attention. Gerontological research has clearly shown the importance of such networks for the elderly in general. This importance is heightened by the realization that, as the next chapter will demonstrate, the alternatives to informal support for many elders living in the farm areas and small towns and villages of this country are often limited by the demographics and economics of rural areas and the urban bias of major formal programs for the aged.

REFERENCES

Adams, B.N. 1968, *Kinship in an Urban Setting*, Markham, Chicago.

Arling, G. 1976, "Resistance to Isolation Among Elderly Widows," *International Journal of Aging and Human Development*, 7, 67–86.

Bengston, U.L., E.B. Olander, and A.A. Haddad. 1976, "The 'Generation Gap' and Aging Family Members: Toward a Conceptualized Model," in J.F. Gubrium (ed.), *Time, Roles, and Self in Old Age*, Human Sciences Press, New York.

Berardo, F.M. 1967, *Social Adaptation to Widowhood Among a Rural/Urban Aged Population*, Agricultural Experiment Bulletin No. 689, College of Agriculture, Washington State University, Pullman, Washington.

Biegel, D.E., and L. Maguire. 1982, "Developing Linkages with Community Support Systems: Limitations and Dangers," paper presented at the Meeting of Community Mental Health Centers, New York.

Britton, J. H., W. Mather, and A. Lansing. 1961, "Expectations for Older Persons in a Rural Community: Living Arrangements and Family Relationships," *Journal of Gerontology*, 1961, 156–162.

Britton, J.H., and Britton, J.O. 1972, *Personality Changes in Aging*, Springer, New York.

Brody, E. 1978, *Long Term Care of Older People: A Practical Guide*, Human Sciences Press, New York.

Bultena, G. 1969, "Rural-Urban Differences in the Familial Interaction of the Aged," *Rural Sociology*, 34, 5–15.

Bultena, G., E. Powers, P. Falkman, and D. Frederick. 1971, *Life After Seventy in Iowa: A Restudy of the Aged*, Sociology Report No. 95, Iowa State University, Ames, Iowa.

Cantor, M. 1975, "Life Space and the Social Support System of the Inner City Elderly of New York," *The Gerontologist*, 15, 23–27.

———. 1979, Neighbors and Friends: An Overlooked Resource in the Informal Support System, *Research on Aging*, 1, 434–463.

Coward, R.T. 1981, "The Other Side of the Coin: Cautions About the Role of Natural Helping Networks in Programs for the Rural Elderly," unpublished manuscript, Burlington, Vermont.

Cryns, A., and C. Nowak. 1981, *Erie County's Elderly Needs Assessment, Preliminary Data Report*, Center for the Study of Aging, SUNY-Buffalo, Buffalo, New York.

Cummings, E., and D. Schneider. 1966, "Sibling Solidarity: A Property of American Kinship," in *Kinship and Family Organization*, B. Barber (ed.), John Wiley and Sons, New York.

Dean, A., and N. Lin. 1977, "The Stress-Buffering Role of Social Support," *Journal of Nervous and Mental Disease*, 165, 403–417.

Deimling, G., and L. Huber. 1981, "The Availability and Participation of Immediate Kin in Caring for the Rural Elderly," paper presented at the annual meeting of the Gerontological Society of America, Toronto, Canada, November 8–12.

Dinkel, R. 1984, "Attitudes of Children Toward Supporting Aged Parents," *American Sociological Review*, 9, 370–379.

Goodfellow, M. 1983, *Reasons for Use and Non-Use of Social Services Among the Rural Elderly*, Pennsylvania State University, University Park, Pa.

Heller, P. 1970, "Familism Scale: A Measure of Family Solidarity," *Journal of Marriage and the Family*, 32, 73–80.

———. 1976, "Familism Scale: Revalidation and Revision," *Journal of Marriage and the Family*, 38, 423–429.

House, J. 1981, *Work Stress and Social Support*, Addison-Wesley Publishers, Reading, Massachusetts.

Johnson, C.L. 1982, "Sibling Solidarity: Its Origin and Functioning in Italian-American Families," *Journal of Marriage and the Family*, 44, 155–167.

Kaplan, B., and D. Fleisher. 1981, "Are Neighbors a Viable Support System for the Frail Elderly?" paper presented at the annual meeting of the Gerontological Society of America, Toronto, November.

Kivett, V.R. 1976, *The Aged in North Carolina: Physical, Social, and Environmental Characteristics and Sources of Assistance*, North Carolina Agricultural Experiment Station, North Carolina State University, April.

———. 1983, "Consanguinity and Kin Level: Their Relative Importance to the Helping Networks of Older Adults," paper presented at the annual meeting of the Gerontological Society of America, San Francisco, California, November.

———. 1985, "Aging in Rural Society: Non-Kin Community Relations and Participation," in *The Elderly in Rural Society*, R.T. Coward and G.R. Lee (eds.), Springer, New York.

Kivett, V.R., and J.R. Scott. 1979, *The Rural By-Passed Elderly*, Technical Bulletin No. 260, North Carolina Agricultural Research Service, University of North Carolina at Greensboro, Greensboro, North Carolina.

Krout, J.A. 1984, *The Utilization of Formal and Informal Support of the Aged: Rural Versus Urban Differences*, final report to the Andrus Foundation, American Association of Retired Persons, Fredonia, New York.

Laurie, W. 1978, *Employing the Duke OARS Methodology in Cost Comparisons: Home Services and Institutionalization*, Duke University Center Reports on Advances in Research, No. 2, Duke University, Durham, North Carolina, Summer.

Lee, G.R. 1980, "Kinship in the Seventies: A Decade Review of Research and Theory," *Journal of Marriage and the Family*, 42, 923–934.

Lee, G.R., and M.L. Cassidy. 1985, "Family and Kin Relations of the Rural Elderly," in *The Elderly in Rural Society*, R. Coward and G. Lee (eds.), Springer, New York.

Lopata, H.Z. 1973, *Widowhood in an American City*, Schenkman Publishing, Cambridge, Massachusetts.

———. 1978, "Contributions of Extended Families to the Support Systems of Metropolitan Area Widows: Limitations of the Modified Kin Network," *Journal of Marriage and the Family*, 40, 355–364.

———. 1979, *Women as Widows*, Elsevier, New York.

McKain, W. 1967, "Community Roles and Activities of Older Rural Persons," in *Older Rural Americans*, E.G. Youmans (ed.), University of Kentucky Press, Lexington, Kentucky.

Mercier, J.M., and E.A. Powers. 1984, "The Family and Friends of Rural Aged as a Natural Support System," *Journal of Community Psychology*, 12, 334–346.

Milgrim, S. 1970, "The Experience of Living In Cities," *Science*, 167, 1461–1468.

Montgomery, J. 1965, *Social Characteristics of the Aged in a Small Pennsylvania Community*, College of Home Economics Research Publication No. 233, Pennsylvania State University, University Park, Pennsylvania.

Nowak, C. 1982, "Informal Networks of Support in Later Life: Conceptual, Methodological, and Applied Rural Versus Urban Issues," paper presented at the annual meeting of the National Conference on the Aging, Washington, D.C., April.

Pastorello, T. 1974, "The Differential Impact of Familial and Non-Familial Close Social Relationships on Morale in Later Life," paper presented at the Annual Meeting of the Gerontological Society of America, Portland, Oregon, October.

Pihlblad, C.T., and R.L. McNamara. 1965, "Social Adjustment of Elderly People in Three Small Towns," in *Older People and Their Social World*, A. Rose and W. Peterson (eds.), F.A. Davis, Philadelphia.

Powers, E., P. Keith, and W. Goudy. 1975, "Family Relationships and Friendships," in *Rural Environments and Aging*, R.C. Atchley and T.O. Byerts (eds.), Gerontological Society, Washington, D.C.

————. 1981, "Family Networks of the Rural Aged," in *The Family in Rural Society*, R. Coward and W. Smith (eds.), Westview Press, Boulder, Colorado.

Powers, R., and M. Liston. 1971, *A Study of the Patterns of Living of the Elderly in Iowa Non-Urban Population Centers*, Bulletin No. 65, Home Economics Research Institute, Ames, Iowa.

Rosenburg, G.S. 1976, "Age, Poverty, and Isolation from Friends in the Urban Working Class," in *Contemporary Social Gerontology*, B.A. Bell (ed.), Charles C. Thomas, Springfield, Illinois.

Rosencranz, H., C.T. Pihlblad, and T. McNevin. 1968, *Social Participation of Older People in the Small Town*, Department of Sociology, University of Missouri, Columbia, Missouri.

Rosow, J. 1967, *Social Interaction of the Aged*, Free Press, New York.

Sauer, W.J., W. Seelbach, and S. Hanson. 1980, "Rural/Urban and Cohort Differences in Filial Responsibility," *Journal of Minority Aging*, 5, 229–305.

Schooler, K. 1975, "A Comparison of Rural and Non-Rural Elderly on Selected Variables," in *Rural Environments and Aging*, R.C. Atchley and T.O. Byerts (eds.), Gerontological Society, Washington, D.C.

Scott, J.P. 1981, *Older Rural Adults: Perspectives on Status and Needs: A Progress Report*, Department of Home and Family Life, Texas Tech University, Lubbock, Texas.

Shanas, E. 1979, "Social Myth as Hypothesis: The Case of the Family Relations of Old People," *The Gerontologist*, 19, 3–19.

Shanas, E., P. Townsend, D. Wedderburn, D. Fries, P. Milhoj, and J. Stewhouwer. 1968, *Old People in Three Industrial Societies*, Atherton Press, New York.

U.S. Bureau of the Census. 1981, *Marital Status and Living Arrangements*, Current Population Reports, Series P–20, No. 316, Table 1, U.S. Government Printing Office, Washington, D.C.

Wade, S., and M. Sporakowski. 1972, "An Intergenerational Comparison of Attitudes Towards Supporting Aged Parents," *Journal of Marriage and the Family*, 34, 42–48.

Ward, R.A. 1978, "Limitations of the Family as a Supportive Institution in the Lives of the Aged," *Family Coordinator*, 27, 365–372.

Wirth, L. 1936, "Urbanism as a Way of Life," *American Journal of Sociology*, 44, 1–24.

Youmans, E.G. 1963, *Aging Patterns in a Rural and an Urban Area of Kentucky*, Bulletin No. 681, Agricultural Experiment Station, Lexington, Kentucky.

———. 1977, "The Rural Aged," *The Annals of the American Academy of Political Science*, 429, 81–90.

9 FORMAL SERVICES AND SERVICE PROVISION

INTRODUCTION

A bewildering array of publicly supported programs and services for the elderly exist in America. In fact, almost every layer of government, as well as many components of the private sector, is in the business of funding, administering, or directly providing service programs to the elderly. While the exact number of governmental units involved in what Estes (1980) has labeled the "aging enterprise" is not easily determined, Soldo (1980) argues that some 135 to 200 federal government programs affect the elderly in some way—either through providing services directly or making available cash assistance or in-kind transfers. It has often been charged that no real system of services for the elderly exists, but rather that programs tend to be fragmented, uncoordinated, and duplicative (Estes, 1980; Soldo, 1980). At the federal level, the authorization for many of these services and programs comes mainly from two pieces of legislation: the Social Security Act and the Older Americans Act. The Older Americans Act in particular has provided direction and funding for a wide array of social and health-related services.

The preceding chapters have examined specific aspects of the rural elderly and their situations. It has been suggested that the rural elderly are more disadvantaged than their urban counterparts in areas such as economic status, housing, and public transportation. And while the existing literature does not provide clear support for rural shortcomings in areas such as health status, it has been pointed out time and time again that rural areas lack the quantity, quality, and comprehensiveness of services found in urban places. Further, it has been noted in previous chapters that the provision of services in rural areas must differ from service delivery in urban areas because of the ecological, organizational, and economic features of these places and the attitudes and characteristics of the rural elderly themselves. Thus, lower population densities of rural areas and the concomitant lack of public transportation combine with the more limited economic and organizational resources to make the delivery of needed services more difficult and costly.

The purpose of this chapter is to discuss, in detail, issues of service availability, accessibility, delivery, and utilization in regard to the rural elderly. The availability of various services and the reasons for the rural disadvantage in this area will be examined. A number of topics generally subsumed under the heading "accessibility" will also be explored. These topics include geographic distance, awareness of services, and attitudes toward services. Rural/urban differences in the degree of use of services and the correlates of this use will then be discussed, with special attention focused on the barriers to such utilization. Finally, alternatives to traditional (i.e., urban-oriented) service delivery modes that are more realistic given the characteristics and resources of rural areas and elderly populations will be explored.

SERVICE AVAILABILITY

As has been noted in earlier chapters, fewer health and social services are available to the elderly living in rural as opposed to urban areas. A number of studies using different samples and methodologies illustrate this rural disadvantage. Taietz and Milton (1979) conducted a study of the number of services offered by 53 upstate New York county offices for the aging. Categorizing counties with at least 50 percent of their population residing in places of 2,500 or less as rural, the authors collected data in 1967 and again in 1976. Urban counties were found to offer a larger number of services at both dates, but the gap had decreased considerably over time. The mean number of services offered increased from 3.2 to 21.8 in rural and from 7.9 to 27.9 in urban counties. The authors attributed the increase for both types of counties to increases in federal funding for services for the elderly.

Despite the impressive increase in services offered by the rural offices for the aging, they still lagged behind the urban counties significantly. All but two of the twenty-five services noted at both dates were offered by a greater percentage of urban counties in 1976. And five of the services (special adult education courses, senior centers, preretirement courses, foster homes service, and media features) were more than twice as likely to be offered in urban versus rural counties. At the same time, rural/urban differences in a number of major elderly services (information and referral, home health aides, home services, homemaker services, and visiting nurses) were reduced considerably (Taietz and Milton, 1979).

A similar study of service availability for a national sample of area agencies on aging conducted by Nelson (1980) confirms the rural/urban differences reported for New York. Using data for 1976–77, Nelson (1980) found that rural agencies provided a more limited range of services than urban agencies. Out of a total of 14 different services, the mean number offered by rural agencies was 4.7 versus 6.1 for urban agencies. A greater percentage of urban than rural agencies offered each of the services except employment/education. Further, rural agencies were three times as likely to offer only one to three services (40 percent versus 14 percent) and almost half as likely to offer eight to twelve services (23 percent versus 39 percent). Rural areas were also much less likely to offer the following: day care, foster care, health-related, homemaker, legal, meals, and protective services (Nelson, 1980). While the comparability of these findings and those reported by Taietz and Milton (1979) for New York suffers due to the use of different service categories, it would appear that the rural/urban convergence for major services reported for New York may not be a national phenomenon.

Both the Taietz and Milton (1979) and Nelson (1980) studies report data from the mid 1970's for area agencies on aging.

Clearly, other organizations are involved in the provision of services to the elderly, and the possibility remains that the last decade has seen another closing of the rural/urban service gap. To explore this possibility, the author recently conducted a 31-state survey of 755 senior centers stratified for community size and region to examine, among other things, rural/urban differences in the availability of senior center activities and services (Krout, 1983a).

This study provided for a fourfold community size typology: nonmetropolitan county less than 5,000, nonmetropolitan county 5,000 and up, metropolitan non–central-city, and metropolitan central city. The data collected for this study reveal that, as was the case for area agencies, rural senior centers offer fewer services than urban senior centers (Krout, 1983a). The total mean number of services offered in each category was 15.6, 17.7, 18.7, and 18.5 respectively. Thus, while not large, community size differentials are apparent, with suburban senior centers offering the highest number of services. Centers located in nonmetropolitan places of less than 5,000 reported offering a significantly smaller number of services in the areas of center access, income supplement, special services, information and referral, and personal counseling, but not in the health and nutrition and in-home areas. Further, the data revealed that the rural centers offering services made them available less frequently than urban centers (Krout, 1983a).

These data on senior centers provide a broader base on which to make generalizations as to rural/urban differences in service availability for the elderly. It would be ill advised to underplay their significance, as senior centers have evolved to play an important role in the senior services delivery network. In fact, the 1978 amendments to the Older Americans Act specify that senior centers should be given attention by area agencies on aging as "focal points" for comprehensive service delivery (Leanse, 1981). In many small towns where they are found, senior centers may be the *only* point for service delivery.

THE RURAL SERVICE DISADVANTAGE

Perhaps the most obvious, but by no means the only, reason for the smaller number of services found in rural areas is lack of funds. A major review of rural/urban differences in services/ program funding not surprisingly reveals that rural areas receive fewer federal dollars both in absolute figures and in proportion to their share of the nation's older population (Ecosometrics, 1981). Kim (1981) concludes that federal governmental programs systematically discriminate against the rural elderly. In terms of the number, scope, and funding levels of programs, urban areas consistently receive a disproportionately larger share of federal resources. Such inequities stretch across all areas: income, maintenance, transportation, housing, health, and mental health.

Kim (1981) cites some examples of this inequity in specific program areas. One-quarter of the dollars spent under Medicare go to rural areas, where two-thirds of the Medicare recipients live. More than three-quarters of the federal housing outlays go to metropolitan areas, and on a per capita basis, rural residents get 41 percent less of these housing expenditures. The Department of Health, Education, and Welfare spent only 14.3 percent of its monies in rural areas.

The limiting effect of these lower rural outlays on service availability is obvious—fewer dollars, less availability and comprehensiveness of services. But the lack of funds does not stem solely from disproportionate federal expenditures. It is compounded by the relative inability of rural areas to provide local funding or seek extra local support. The lower tax base and higher poverty levels of rural places reduce their ability to generate local matching funds or support programs independently (Ecosometrics, 1981).

However, it is not simply lack of money that restricts the availability of services for the elderly in rural places. Numerous studies have detailed the shortage of trained professionals and paraprofessionals in rural America (New York State Senate, 1980; U.S. Department of Agriculture, 1980; U.S. Department of Health, Education and Welfare, 1975). A rural "person power" shortage is found for many occupations: physicians, dentists, and nurses (Ahearn, 1979), social workers (Munson, 1980), mental health workers (Wagenfeld and Wagenfeld, 1981), psychiatrists (National Institute of Mental Health, 1973), and psychologists (Keller et al., 1980). This shortage of professionals may be caused by a number of factors, including the historic out-migration of young people to metropolitan areas and the lack of adequate facilities, resources, and support mechanisms necessary to attract professionals (Ecosometrics, 1981).

In addition and related to this lack of funding and professionals is the underlying degree of community structure and organizational complexity of rural areas. Several authors (Noll, 1978; Steinhauer, 1980) have noted that rural places are not characterized by the structural complexity necessary to support specialized services. This problem is exacerbated by a lack of coordination both within and between communities and the public and private sectors that reduces the comprehensibility of services (New York State Senate, 1980). Finally, it has been argued that the strong attitudes of self-support and mistrust of government services among rural populations result in a reluctance among local officials to develop programs (Ecosometrics, 1981).

Few studies provide direct rural/urban comparisons of service availability, and very little if any research has investigated the relative importance of factors such as funding levels, manpower levels, community complexity, agency coordination, and community attitudes. The author's (Krout, 1983a) research on community size differences in senior center service availability, however, does provide some insight into this question. Multiple regression analysis reveals that community size per se is not related to the number of services offered by senior centers. Rather, the characteristics of the center users (percentage nonwhite and aged 75 and over) and the center itself (size of budget, number of paid and volunteer staff, and complexity of organizations) are positively related to center services. Thus, the smaller budgets and staff of rural senior centers and user characteristics account for the rural service disadvantage. It is these factors and not necessarily rural location per se that are associated with service availability. Presumably, centers in more populated areas with smaller budgets and staff also have smaller service offerings. Rural centers in general have considerably smaller budgets and staff and are much less likely to be part of multisite organizations (Krout, 1983a).

SERVICE ACCESSIBILITY

It goes without saying that a major impediment to service accessibility (the ability of people to make use of available services) is the low density and geographic dispersion of rural populations that results in greater distances between people and service sites. In fact, Parkinson (1981, 227) states that physical distance "represents the most formidable barrier to the development of programs for rural areas . . . and complicates the delivery of every service and often removes the rural elderly from life's basic necessities." While distance or time/effort/cost to get to a service can be problematic for the urban elderly, it is especially so for the rural aged. An earlier study by the author in western New York (Krout and Larson, 1980) found that getting to services was the foremost problem for a sample of nonmetropolitan elderly, and Schooler (1975) reports that 82 percent of the rural versus 10 percent of the urban elderly in a national sample reported themselves to be far from a set of core services. And these greater distances have impacts on service utilization. Windley (1983) reports that use of 15 community services for elderly residents of 18 small Kansas towns was inversely related with distance to services.

The problem of distance is heightened by terrain and weather (Ambrosius, 1981) and by the paucity of public transportation in rural areas. As was noted in the chapter on transportation, the rural elderly are more likely to own a vehicle than the urban elderly. But the greater distances traveled in rural areas make the costs associated with the use of such vehicles greater. Those elderly who do not own a vehicle or cannot afford to use it must rely on relatives and friends and thus risk giving up part of the all-important feeling of independence and self-reliance or use the usually non-existent public or commercial transportation. The problem of getting people to services or services to people creates obstacles for service funding and is one of the greatest impediments to meeting the needs of the rural elderly.

SERVICE UTILIZATION

Services for the elderly are both less available and less accessible in rural areas. These facts would suggest that the actual utilization of services would be lower in rural than urban areas as well. Unfortunately, few studies have examined rural/urban differences in this regard, and fewer still have adopted research designs that allow an identification of the degree of or reasons for such differences. A number of researchers (Auerbach, 1976; Osgood, 1977; Powers and Bultena, 1974) report lower rural than urban service utilization rates. The author (Krout, 1983b) found slightly higher rates for urban (2,500 and up) as opposed to rural elderly residing in a western New York nonmetropolitan county. Not all studies have found higher rates for the urban elderly. For example, May et al. (1976) report no rural/urban differences for participation in a nutrition program, and Taietz (1970) found considerably greater participation in senior centers for the rural elderly. In fact, Taietz found the percentage of elderly attending senior centers declined progressively from 26 percent for places of less than 2,500 to 4 percent for suburban and central city dwellers.

The findings from a more recent study by the author illustrate the need for more sophisticated analysis and comparative data (Krout, 1984). In a study carried out in both a nonmetropolitan and metropolitan county in western New York, the metropolitan sample was more likely to use all of the following services: home help, home health, elderly visitors, information/referral, home meals, hot luncheon sites, transportation, and legal aid. However, when the nonmetropolitan and metropolitan samples were broken down further into rural/urban and suburban/central city categories respectively, the residential difference became less clear. The nonmetropolitan rural group had the highest percentage of users for the hot luncheon program and had utilization rates very close to the suburban and central city groups for three other services (home meals, home health, and information/referral). The nonmetropolitan urban sample (2,500 and up), however, had considerably lower rates of use for these services. In addition, when the community size variable was entered into a multiple regression analysis, it was not found to be significantly related to a summed service utilization score (Krout, 1984).

These findings indicate several things. First, considerable variation may exist in service utilization rates for the elderly living in different sized "rural" communities. Second, while rural/urban differences may indeed exist, an important and largely unanswered question is the relative importance of community size as a predictor of service use. Third, the existing research is largely limited to geographically restricted samples. Finally, it should be stressed that the elderly in general tend to turn to formal services for certain kinds of needs (health) and to informal sources for other needs (general shopping, household tasks).

Attitudes Toward Service Use

It should be noted that the elderly in general do not desire to utilize formal (publicly supported) services. Independence and self-reliance are basic and important conditions the elderly hold dear, and the use of social or health service is seen by many elderly as an admission that they cannot take care of themselves and must rely on the government. Moen (1978), in fact, reports that not only are the elderly reluctant to admit need or seek help, but they may even go so far as to deny using services. When assistance is needed, most elderly prefer to rely on family or friends (Cantor, 1977).

It is often argued that the rural elderly's adherence to values of independence and self-reliance is particularly strong (Coward, 1979). This in turn leads to an unwillingness to accept service programs as legitimate and further complicates the provision of such services to the rural elderly (Auerbach, 1976; Buxton, 1976; Karcher and Karcher, 1980; Osgood, 1977). While this point is well taken, the existing research does not allow a determination as to whether or not this orientation is greater among the rural versus the urban elderly. In addition, not all studies conclude that attitudes toward independence inhibit the rural elderly from using services. Goodfellow (1983) writes that the rural elderly in a Pennsylvania sample report not using formal services because they did not feel they needed them, not because they wanted to keep their independence. The author (Krout, 1983c) has noted that there is little work that actually examines the role such attitudes play in the use of services in rural versus urban settings. And as Coward and Rathbone-McCuan (1985) point out, previous work has not included appropriate rural/urban samples, controlled for important variables such as need or personal characteristics, or considered the impact of the nature or delivery mode of particular services on their acceptability to the elderly.

Service Awareness

In addition to values and attitudes toward services, a fundamental factor affecting service utilization is awareness of services. In fact, Fowler (1970) argues that lack of program awareness is the most important determinant of the under-utilization of services by the elderly. What can be said of rural/urban differences in service awareness among the elderly? A number of factors would lead one to expect lower levels of service awareness among the rural elderly. As was noted earlier, several studies have reported that a supposed primary source of program awareness, information and referral services, is less available in rural areas (Ecosometrics, 1981; Krout, 1983b; Nelson, 1980). Rural places are also seen as presenting additional obstacles to the provision of information and referral services. These include less adequate telephone systems, a greater proportion of homes without phones, and larger service areas that may require long-distance calls (Coward and Rathbone-McCuan, 1985). And Hayslip et al. (1980) argue that the greater physical and social isolation and poor health of the rural elderly reduce the likelihood of their knowing about (or utilizing) available home care services in particular.

Research on the general elderly population's awareness of services is unequivocal, with findings on the degree of knowledge of medical and social services varying considerably from study to study and service to service (Krout, 1983a). For example, Lopata (1975) reports that 10 percent of a sample of Chicago elderly were aware of an information center for senior citizens, while Downing (1957) found two-thirds of a Syracuse, New York, sample aware of a senior club. However, relatively few studies have examined awareness levels for the rural elderly, and fewer still have carried out rural/urban comparisons.

Data from a study by the author (Krout and Larson, 1980) on the elderly in a New York nonmetropolitan county indicate that a fairly large percentage of elderly had "heard of" service programs. Approximately two-thirds had heard of four services (luncheon clubs, senior clubs and centers, mini-buses, and Medicaid), while roughly one-third were aware of homemaker services and an information/referral service. Kivett (1976) reports varying levels of awareness for different services for a sample of North Carolina nonmetropolitan elderly. For example, two-thirds of her sample had heard of senior citizens' clubs, slightly over one-half had heard of meals on wheels, and 40 percent were aware of a home health aid service. Kivett and Scott (1979), however, report higher levels of awareness for another North Carolina sample for senior clubs, homemaker services, and home health aid service.

A more recent study by the author (Krout, 1984) presents one of the few rural/urban comparisons of service awareness. Data from 600 elderly living in a range of western New York communities indicate that community size was positively related to a summed service awareness score. While 25 percent of the elderly in rural and urban nonmetropolitan places were aware of from five to eight of eight services, 44 percent of the metropolitan sample was so aware. In fact, community size was the strongest predictor of the overall service awareness score. Unfortunately, there is a scarcity of other data with which to compare these results. In addition, little is known about the correlates of service awareness for the rural elderly. Earlier work by the author (Krout and Larson, 1980) for a sample of nonmetropolitan elderly found that those who were better educated, female, and married were aware of more social programs. Other studies of the elderly in general have not found these factors to be as important as income (Snider, 1980).

OTHER FACTORS RELATED TO SERVICE UTILIZATION

While accessibility, acceptability, and awareness of services are all significantly related to their use, other factors can be expected to have an impact on whether or not individuals utilize services. Indeed, a longitudinal study by Powers and Bultena (1974) found a considerable lack of congruity between attitudes toward services and the use of those services and concluded that the level of awareness of services did not explain use, as many elderly who were aware of services did not use them. A number of studies with samples of rural elderly report low levels of use for those aware (Kivett, 1976; Kivett and Scott, 1979; Krout, 1983b, 1984). What factors might differentiate service users from non-users?

As the author has noted in a review of the service utilization literature (Krout, 1983c), social gerontologists have by and large restricted their analyses to an examination of how socio-demographic factors affect this phenomenon. As a result, the literature on correlates of use is largely descriptive and provides little more than a catalog of the socio-economic characteristics that differentiate users from non-users. This does not provide much insight as to *why* such connections exist or into the complex interplay of individual attitudes and motivations, interactional processes, and structural factors that affect the service participation process. In addition, the findings of service utilization research are inconsistent and often contradictory (Krout, 1983c).

This is true for studies of rural elderly service utilization as well. For example, Cottrell (1975) found use of a publicly supported transportation system for the elderly in rural Ohio greater for females, those living alone, and those over age 70. A study of a sample of nonmetropolitan elderly by the author (Krout, 1983b) found that marital status, age, and income but not sex were related to the number of services used. The correlates of use did vary somewhat depending on the service under investigation. It is also interesting to note that other research has found that a large majority of the rural elderly may not turn to formal agencies for support because they do not need "outside" help (Mansfield et al., 1983). These authors report that the nature of the support depended on the nature of the need and that the rural elderly in two small Pennsylvania towns relied on formal agencies mainly for health-related assistance. Yet Goodfellow (1983) found that contact with informal supports was positively associated with service use and that informal networks served as links to the bureaucracy and provided information about programs, a finding also noted by Daatland (1983).

PROBLEMS IN THE DELIVERY OF SERVICES

It has been noted that rural areas have fewer services for the elderly and that the more dispersed patterns of population distribution and lack of public transportation create problems of accessibility that result in lower rates of use. These problems of availability and accessibility are compounded by the strong resistance that many rural elderly have to using such programs. Karcher and Karcher (1980) argue that rural "subcultural" values and attitudes (emphasis on self-reliance, reluctance to admit need, and mistrust of government officials) contribute significantly to the limited success of rural elderly service programs. The literature contains a number of analyses that point out in detail the weaknesses and problems inhibiting the development and execution of programs for the rural elderly.

Steinhauer (1980) cites the following as contributing to the overall inadequacy of rural service delivery systems: lack of full-time administrative professionals in rural governments, inability of rural areas to meet federal matching requirements, lack of adequate service infrastructure (personnel and organizational), higher costs due to greater distances, and inappropriate use of urban service models. The New York State Senate (1980) report on the rural elderly identifies many of the same kinds of problems but places them in three categories of weaknesses that characterize human service delivery systems in rural America: policy-based, program-based, and community-based.

Local offices of the aging charged with coordinating existing services in a comprehensive manner face considerable obstacles because of these problems. Besides the cold fact that there are often few services to coordinate, sheer distance between populations creates additional problems in matching clients with services. For example, Means et al. (1978) report that one-half of a sample of rural elderly who did not use social services and programs cited a lack of transportation as a reason. But transportation is not the only problem in service provision or coordination. The author's recent national survey of senior centers (Krout 1983a) asked center directors to indicate barriers to working with other service agencies. Approximately one-quarter of the nonmetropolitan center directors cited lack of transportation/ communication/understanding and over one-third cited lack of time as barriers to such coordination. A special New York State Office for the Aging (1982) study of barriers to the coordination and delivery of services to the rural elderly revealed the following as the most important barriers: unavailability and lack of coordination of transportation, a lack of health services (especially home health care), and a lack of coordination in both the planning and delivery of services.

PROVIDING SERVICES IN RURAL SETTINGS

Several scholars (Coward, 1977, 1979; Ginsberg, 1976, 1981) have argued that the delivery of services in rural settings should differ significantly from large urban locales. Coward (1977) notes that rural areas require more than a watered-down version of large-city programs. Further, Kerckhoff and Coward (1977) argue that research on the rural elderly reveals five major factors that should be considered in the development and delivery of services to the rural elderly. These include the existence of a large diversity within and between rural communities, the existence of a considerable age diversity within the rural elderly, the need to recognize that there are many myths about the rural elderly (such as super-strong extended family ties) that must be discarded, the need to establish ties with existing community units, and the importance of including the elderly's "significant others" in the service delivery process.

Coward et al. (1983) have identified distinctive characteristics of rural environments that call for different service provision practices and strategies. These characteristics are grouped into three major categories and include features of rural client populations (demographics, attitudes/beliefs/values, educational status, economic patterns, and physical and mental health status), features of the social and physical environment (topography and terrain, population distribution, cultural enclaves, community organization and services, and housing), and features of the provision of rural services (educational preparation, training, knowledge, skills, attributes, and values of providers, and task environment).

These observations are extremely useful and can serve as a basis for a systematic examination and development of service delivery alternatives for the rural elderly. Up to now, analyses of unique service provision problems in regard to the rural elderly have generally not been translated into workable ideas or incorporated into the existing framework of services for the elderly. Perhaps the most common (and an effective) service strategy has been to make various services mobile and bring them to the rural elderly in their communities. This is being done with services such as health screening (Bell, 1976), information and referral (Ecosometrics, 1981), and recreational facilities (National Council on the Aging, 1975). Mobile service units reduce costs and are highly visible and in essence do their own outreach work (New York State Senate, 1980). Other rural adaptations include "circuit-riding professionals" (Bigel, 1979).

Finally, senior centers have been identified as being particularly well suited to assist in the delivery and coordination of a wide range of services in rural areas (New York State Senate, 1980) and can be central to a comprehensive approach to local service delivery (Wozny and Burkhardt, 1980). Ott (1977) argues that senior centers do not carry a "welfare stigma" and can increase the rural elderly's service awareness by serving as a focal point for a variety of services (New York State Senate, 1980). In fact, several studies of rural services have reported relatively high rates of use for senior centers (Krout, 1983b; Scott, 1983). However, the author's recent national study indicates that rural senior centers differ widely in the availability of programs and have fewer personnel and fewer financial and organizational resources than urban centers (Krout, 1984). It is important to note that without sufficient outreach efforts and transportation services, rural senior centers run the risk of serving a very small segment of the most needy elderly population (Leatherman and Grinstead-Schneider, 1980).

RESEARCH NEEDS

It is clear from the preceding discussion that many important issues remain unresolved regarding the delivery of services to the rural elderly. While the literature indicates quite clearly that the services for the rural elderly are less available, less accessible, less comprehensive, and face considerable barriers in their provision, the existing research has not pursued these issues systematically. There is a dearth of well conceived and well executed comparative work and a corresponding lack of data that would allow generalizations as to the relative importance of various factors in explaining, predicting, and ultimately resolving service delivery questions.

Perhaps the most basic question in need of more systematic research is that of how residential location interacts with other variables that have been identified in previous research as related to service use and delivery issues. Little is known about this because existing service awareness and utilization studies suffer from substantial shortcomings (Krout, 1983c) and because residence has rarely been examined in multivariate studies with adequate sampling designs. As Coward and Rathbone-McCuan (1985) note, the interaction of individual factors such as attitudes and needs with environmental factors such as community resources and physical barriers has largely been ignored.

Important and unanswered question exist for virtually every issue examined in this chapter. It has been noted that there is a significant shortage of services in rural areas. However, little research has been carried out on the relative importance of various service needs and how these needs can be most effectively met. It has been suggested that urban service delivery models cannot simply be transported to rural areas and that rural differences in population characteristics and social and physical environments require different professional skills and service provision modes (Coward et al., 1983). Recognizing this, gerontologists must move on. Many rural service provision agencies have developed strategies for dealing with resource shortages and dispersed populations, but there is scant attention paid to these by gerontologists. Program descriptions, comparisons, and evaluations must be conducted if rural agencies are to do the best job possible.

Closely related to the issue of how many and what kinds of services are made available to the rural elderly are questions of their quality and cost. Very few studies have been carried out on the effectiveness or quality of services (Krout, 1984), although existing research would suggest poorer quality in rural areas (Coward and Rathbone-McCuan, 1985). Likewise, there have been few rural/urban comparisons of service cost, and the results of these have been equivocal (Ecosometrics, 1981). As Coward and Rathbone-McCuan (1985) point out, the answer to rural/ urban differences in service cost has serious implications for policy issues involving funding allocations and formulas and is in need of much more attention.

Specific issues such as the problems related to service accessibility need to be investigated further. For example, lack of service accessibility for the rural elderly has been tied to a number of factors, such as awareness, client eligibility, administrative practices, and fiscal and psychological constraints (Ecosometrics, 1981). But little is known about the relative impact of each, how a particular change in one would affect the others, and the result such changes would have on the demand for and use of a particular service. Likewise, it has been noted that awareness of services among the rural elderly is relatively low. This suggests that present mechanisms for informing the rural elderly about programs are ineffective and/or inappropriate. Much work needs to be done on rural/urban differences in levels and correlates of service awareness and to determine more effective ways of getting information to potential users.

Questions concerning the rural elderly's utilization of services exist as well. More rural/urban comparisons are needed to determine who uses services and why. Many authors argue that the rural elderly are more likely to have problems in areas such as health, housing, and income. Therefore, a basic question is, under what conditions do the rural elderly act on those problems and turn to the formal service delivery system for assistance? In other words, when, why, and how is a need translated into a demand for service? Do existing services meet current demands or needs? How many rural elderly with a particular kind of need do not use existing services and why? What kinds of changes in service availability and accessibility would produce increases or decreases in service use and why? The answers to these and other questions are basic to building effective responses to the needs of the rural elderly.

SUMMARY

This chapter has examined the availability, accessibility, utilization, and provision of services to the rural elderly. While these topics have been discussed for specific areas throughout this book, the purpose of this chapter was to develop a more general overview of service-related issues. Many of the preceding chapter summaries have stated that too little of the right kind of information exists to draw firm conclusions as to the status or circumstances of the rural elderly. Even though significant gaps in the literature on services have been identified, it is clear that the rural elderly suffer a distinct service disadvantage when compared with their urban counterparts. This disadvantage appears whether one is talking about the number, scope, accessibility, or adequacy of services.

Rural areas offer fewer services to their elderly residents partly because per capita federal allocations to rural programs are smaller. In addition, rural places generally have smaller tax bases. This lack of money is compounded by a shortage of personnel and organizational resources as well. In essence, rural areas generally do not have the infrastructure necessary to support extensive formal service networks. The shortcomings in service availabiliiy are exacerbated by problems of accessibility. The geographic dispersion of rural elderly populations, combined with non-existent or inadequate transportation systems, creates formidable barriers to the provision and utilization of elderly services. These and other factors contribute to lower levels of service awareness and utilization.

It is clear that numerous problems face those who would design and implement effective service delivery strategies for the rural elderly. Once again, the ecology of rural environments presents a major obstacle to program coordination and delivery. Yet given the lack of resources, such coordination is not only more crucial in rural than in urban areas, it is often more difficult. A number of scholars have argued forcefully that the characteristics of rural places and the rural elderly require innovative service models and delivery strategies. Watered-down urban programs are usually not appropriate or effective. In addition, federal policies on the aging are urban-oriented and make little effort to address the circumstances found in rural places. Despite the recognition of these factors, significant gaps in the literature inhibit the development of effective responses to these shortcomings. It is imperative that researchers identify the information needed to develop and evaluate effective and responsive service delivery strategies.

The previous chapter has shown that while the informal networks of the rural elderly are indeed strong, they do not assume a much greater role than is the case for the urban elderly. Yet given the lack of formal resources in many rural communities, questions concerning the role that relatives, friends, neighbors, and local organizations do and could play in assisting the elderly take on considerable significance. This is not to suggest that rural informal networks can or should take on activities handled by formal agencies in urban places, but rather to suggest that researchers should investigate more fully how service programs can build on the strengths of rural communities, including informal networks, to increase the degree of service coverage and quality.

To this end, Jacobson, as noted in Ecosometrics (1981), suggests that agency personnel work with informal supports in a number of ways. These include developing training and technical assistance packages to help caregivers provide better care, providing respite services for family members and financial incentives (especially for transportation costs), and developing federal and local agency policies to encourage working with informal caregivers. Coward (1979) further notes that the joining of formal to informal efforts can reduce community resistance to the formal system and produce savings in personnel and "brick and mortar" costs. These and other responses to the service needs of the rural elderly need to be examined carefully. The success of efforts to design, implement, and operate programs consistent with the realities of rural communities and the needs of the rural aged will not only have significant impacts on the lives of those who are elderly today but may well be even more salient for those who will reach the status of elder 20 and 30 years from now.

REFERENCES

Ahearn, M.C. 1979, *Health Care in Rural America*, U.S. Department of Agriculture, Economic, Statistics, and Cooperative Service, Information Bulletin No. 428, U.S. Government Printing Office, Washington, D.C.

Ambrosius, G.R. 1981, "To Dream the Impossible Dream: Delivering Coordinated Services to the Rural Elderly," in *Toward Mental Health of the Rural Elderly*, P. Kim and C. Wilson (eds.), University Press of America, Washington, D.C.

Auerbach, A.J. 1976, "The Elderly in Rural and Urban Areas," in *Social Work in Rural Communities*, L.H. Ginsberg (ed.), Council on Social Work Education, New York.

Bell, B.D. 1975, "Mobile Medical Care to the Elderly," *The Gerontologist*, 15, 100–103.

Bigel, M. 1979, "Legal Services," in *Handbook of Human Services for Older Persons*, I. Holmes (ed.), Human Sciences Press, New York.

Buxton, E.B. 1976, "Delivering Social Services in Rural Areas, in *Social Work in Rural Communities*, L.H. Ginsberg (ed.), Council on Social Work Education, New York.

Cantor, M.H. 1977, "Neighbors and Friends: An Overlooked Resource in the Informal Support System," paper presented at the annual meeting of the Gerontological Society of America, San Francisco, California, November.

Cottrell, F. 1975, "Transportation of the Rural Aged," in *Rural Environments and Aging*, R. Atchley (ed.), Gerontological Society of America, Washington, D.C.

Coward, R.T. 1977, "Delivering Social Services in Small Towns and Rural Communities," in *Rural Families Across the Life Span: Implications for Community Programming*, R.T. Coward (ed.), Indiana Cooperative Extension Service, West Lafayette, Indiana.

———. 1979, "Planning Community Services for the Rural Elderly: Implications for Research," *The Gerontologist*, 19, 275–282.

Coward, R.T., and E. Rathbone-McCuan. 1985, "Delivering Health and Human Services to the Elderly in Rural Society," in *The Elderly in Rural Society*, R. Coward and G. Lee (eds.), Springer, New York.

Coward, R.T., K.L. DeWeaver, F.E. Schmidt, and R.W. Jackson. 1983, "Mental Health Practice in Rural Environments: A Frame of Reference," *The International Journal of Mental Health*, 12, 3–24.

Daatland, S.O. 1983, "Use of Public Services for the Aged and the Role of the Family," *The Gerontologist*, 23, 650–656.

Downing, J. 1957, "Factors Affecting the Selective Use of a Social Club for the Aged," *Journal of Gerontology*, 12, 81–84.

Ecosometrics. 1981, *Review of Reported Differences Between the Rural and Urban Elderly: Status, Needs, Services, and Service Costs*, Administration on Aging (Contract No. 105–80–6–065), Washington, D.C.

Estes, C. 1980, *The Aging Enterprise*, Jossey-Bass, San Francisco.

Fowler, J. 1970, "Knowledge, Need, and Use of Services Among the Aged," in *Health Care Services for the Aged*, C. Osterbind (ed.), University of Florida Press, Gainesville, Florida.

Ginsberg, L.H. 1976, *Social Work in Rural Communities*, Council on Social Work Education, New York.

———. 1981, "Rural Social Work Education," *Arete*, 6, 13–17.

Goodfellow, M. 1983, *Reasons for Use and Nonuse of Social Services Among the Rural Elderly of Pennsylvania*, Pennsylvania State University, University Park, Pennsylvania.

Hayslip, B., et al. 1980, "Home Care Services and the Rural Elderly," *The Gerontologist*, 20, 192–199.

Karcher, E.J., and B.E. Karcher. 1980, "Education and Religion: Potential Partners in Service to the Rural Elderly," *Educational Gerontology: International Quarterly*, 5, 409–421.

Keller, P.A., J.D. Zimbleman, K.K. Murray, and R.N. Feil. 1980, "Geographic Distribution of Psychologists in the Northeastern United States," *Journal of Rural Community Psychology*, 1, 18–24.

Kerckhoff, R.K., and R.T. Coward. 1977, "Delivering Human Services to the Rural Elderly: Implications from Research," paper presented at the annual conference of the National Council on Family Relations, San Diego, California, October.

Kim, P. 1981, "The Low Income Rural Elderly: Under-Served Victims of Public Inequity," in *Toward Mental Health of the Rural Elderly*, P. Kim and C. Wilson (eds.), University Press of America, Washington, D.C.

Kivett, V. 1976, *The Aged in North Carolina: Physical, Social, and Environmental Characteristics and Sources of Assistance*, North Carolina Agricultural Experiment Station, North Carolina State University, Raleigh, North Carolina, April.

Kivett, V., and J. Scott. 1979, *The Rural By-Passed Elderly*, Technical Bulletin No. 260, North Carolina Agricultural Research Service, University of North Carolina at Greensboro, Greensboro, North Carolina.

Krout, J.A. 1983a, *The Organization, Operation, and Programming of Senior Centers: A National Survey*, final report to the Andrus Foundation,

American Association of Retired Persons, Fredonia, New York.
———. 1983b, Correlates of Service Utilization Among the Rural Elderly, *The Gerontologist*, 23, 500–504.
———. 1983c, "Knowledge and Use of Services by the Elderly: A Critical Review of the Literature," *International Journal of Aging and Human Development*, 17, 153–167.
———. 1984, *The Utilization of Formal and Informal Support by the Aged: Rural Versus Urban Differences*, final report to the Andrus Foundation, American Association of Retired Persons, Fredonia, New York.

Krout, J.A., and D. Larson. 1980, "Self-Assessed Needs of the Rural Elderly," paper presented at the annual meeting of the Rural Sociological Society, Guelph, Ontario, August.

Leanse, J. 1981, *Senior Centers: A Focal Point for Delivery of Services*, National Council on the Aging, Washington, D.C.

Leatherman, M.K., and M.J. Grinstead-Schneider. 1980, *Factors Affecting Participation in a Senior Citizens Center, Crawford County, Arkansas*, University of Arkansas, Fayetteville, Arkansas.

Lopata, H. 1975, "Support Systems of Elderly Urbanites: Chicago of the 1970s," *The Gerontologist*, 15, 35–41.

Mansfield, P., et al. 1983, *Preliminary Findings from a Study of Informal Networks, Service Use, and Health Status Among a Sample of Elderly in Two Rural Pennsylvania Communities*, Pennsylvania State University, University Park, Pennsylvania.

May, A., S. Herrman, and J. Fitzgerald. 1976, *An Evaluation of Congregate Meals Programs and Health of Elders: Scott County and Fort Smith, Arkansas*, Bulletin No. 808, University of Arkansas, Fayetteville, Arkansas.

Means, G., J. Mann, and D. VanDyke. 1978, "Reaching Out to the Rural Elderly—Services to Rural America," *Human Services in the Rural Environment*, 3, 1–5.

Moen, E. 1978, "The Reluctance of the Elderly to Accept Help," *Social Problems*, 25, 293–303.

Munson, C.E. 1980, "Urban-Rural Differences: Implications for Education and Training," *Journal of Education for Social Work*, 16, 95.

National Council on the Aging. 1975, *Bringing Services to People in Rural Areas, Senior Centers: Realizing Our Potential*, proceedings of the Eighth National Conference of Senior Centers, National Council on the Aging, Washington, D.C.

National Institute of Mental Health. 1973, *Federally Funded Community Mental Health Centers*, Division of Mental Health Programs, National Institute of Mental Health, Department of Health, Education and Welfare, Washington, D.C.

Nelson G. 1980, "Social Services to the Urban and Rural Aged: The Experience of Area Agencies on Aging," *The Gerontologist*, 20, 200–207.

New York State Office for the Aging. 1982, *Identification of Barriers Report*, Rural Aging Services Project, New York State Office for the Aging, Albany, New York.

New York State Senate. 1980, *Old Age and Ruralism: A Case of Double Jeopardy, Report on the Rural Elderly*, New York State Senate, Albany, New York.

Noll, P.F. 1978, *Federally Assisted Housing Programs for the Elderly in Rural Areas—Programs and Prospects*, Housing Assistance Council, Washington, D.C.

Osgood, M. 1977, "Rural and Urban Attitudes Towards Welfare," *Social Work*, 22, 41–47.

Ott, C. 1977, *For the Sake of the Rural Poor, Rural Human Resources Programs*, National Association of Counties Research Foundation, Washington, D.C.

Parkinson, L. 1981, "Improving the Delivery of Health Services to the Rural Elderly: A Policy Perspective," in *Toward Mental Health of the Rural Elderly*, P. Kim and C. Wilson (eds.), University Press of America, Washington, D.C.

Powers, E., and G. Bultena. 1974, "Correspondence Between Anticipated and Actual Use of Public Services by the Aged," *Social Services Review*, 48, 245–254.

Schooler, K. 1975, "A Comparison of Rural and Non-Rural Elderly on Selected Variables," in *Rural Environments and Aging*, R.C. Atchley and T.O Byerts (eds.), Gerontological Society, Washington, D.C.

Scott, J. 1983, "Older Rural Adults: Perspectives on Status and Needs," paper presented at American Home Economics Association Annual Meeting, Milwaukee, Wisconsin.

Snider, E. 1980, "Awareness and Use of Health in Services by the Elderly: A Canadian Study," *Medical Care*, 18, 1177–1182.

Soldo, B. 1980, "America's Elderly in the 1980's," *Population Bulletin*, 35, 15–18.

Steinhauer, M.B. 1980, "Obstacles to the Mobilization and Provision of Services to the Rural Elderly," *Educational Gerontology: An International Quarterly*, 5, 399–407.

Taietz, P. 1970, *Community Structure and Aging*, Department of Rural Sociology, Cornell University, Ithaca, New York.

Taietz, P., and S. Milton. 1979, "Rural-Urban Differences in the Structure of Services for the Elderly in Upstate New York Counties," *Journal of Gerontology*, 34, 429–437.

U.S. Department of Agriculture and Farmers Home Administration. 1980, *Improving Services for the Rural Elderly*, U.S. Government Printing Office, Washington, D.C.

U.S. Department of Health, Education and Welfare. 1975, *Getting Human Services to Rural America*, U.S. Government Printing Office, Washington, D.C.

Wagenfeld, M.O., and J.K. Wagenfeld. 1981, "Values, Culture, and Delivery of Mental Health Services," in *Perspectives on Rural Mental Health*, M.O. Wagenfeld (ed.), Jossey-Bass, San Francisco.

Windley, P. G. 1983, "Community Services in Small Rural Towns: Patterns of Use by Older Residents," *The Gerontologist*, 23, 180–184.

Wozny, M.C., and J.E. Burkhardt. 1980, *Analysis of the Continuation of Services Funded Under Title III of the Older Americans Act of 1965*, Institute for Economic and Social Measurements, Washington, D.C.

10   SUMMARY AND CONCLUDING REMARKS

SOME SUMMARY OBSERVATIONS

It is difficult to summarize several hundred pages of findings, analyses, and discussion on a topic with as many facets as have been revealed in this examination of the rural elderly. A major and often-repeated observation has been that both the places and elderly populations seen as rural encompass a complex and rich diversity that defies simple categorization or generalization. This caveat notwithstanding, it has been noted that the aged living outside of metropolitan areas do differ on some basic socio-demographic characteristics. They are more likely to be married and not live alone. This is especially true for the farm elderly, particularly elderly female farm dwellers. They are also more likely to be white than their urban counterparts. The studies reviewed here also suggest that the rural elderly have lower incomes, are somewhat less healthy, live in less adequate housing, are more dependent on the private automobile as a means of transportation, experience more transportation-related problems, have fewer services available and accessible to them, and have lower rates of service awareness and utilization. It has also been noted that the nature, degree, and universality of these rural/urban differences have not been clearly demonstrated.

How can these differences, or probable differences, be accounted for? What aspects of rural areas impact significantly on the life circumstances of the rural elderly? The answer to that query is complex indeed. It is suggested here that a number of dimensions of the rural environment have surfaced throughout this analysis as determinants of the status of the rural elderly. These include the values, economy, ecology, demography, and social organization of rural areas. Each of these will be discussed briefly in regard to their consequences for the aged.

First, social scientists continue to debate the degree to which a unique set of values/beliefs/attitudes can be said to characterize rural America. Nonetheless, a number of authors have argued that the rural elderly hold a value structure which differs from the urban elderly in nature and degree. Rural people are characterized as being especially independent, self-reliant, neighborly, family-oriented, hardworking, mistrustful of government, and leary of programs seen as "welfare" or part of the social service bureaucracy. A number of circumstances of the rural versus urban elderly could be seen as related to these values. There is some evidence to suggest that the rural elderly (especially farmers) are more likely to be members of the labor force. They appear to have somewhat higher levels of contact with friends and neighbors. The rural elderly express relatively high levels of life satisfaction and satisfaction with things such as housing, income, and health, even though objective indicators would suggest some rural disadvantage. In addition, the rural elderly evidence lower formal health and social service utilization rates. However, it is quite possible that other aspects of rural areas besides values account partially or completely for these and other rural elderly characteristics.

Second, the economy of rural areas is more likely to be devoted to extractive industries such as agriculture. In addition, while nonmetropolitan areas have experienced considerable growth in some types of manufacturing, by and large these areas have lower wage scales than urban places. It has been suggested that a more gradual retirement is possible in agriculture, which may account for the higher labor force participation rates of rural males. The lower wage scales contribute to the lower incomes of the rural elderly that in turn can have direct impacts on the ability to meet needs in many areas (food, housing, transportation, etc.) and may account for the importance of friends and neighbors in leisure pursuits.

Third, the ecology of rural areas has been referred to time and time again as important for the rural elderly. The smaller population size and density cannot support as large and diverse service structures as urban areas, thus restricting the availability of programs and services in areas such as housing, transportation, health, leisure, etc. The sparseness of population and greater distances between population settlements result in greater travel costs, more limited accessibility to services, and greater potential personal and social isolation. These greater distances may also be a factor in the somewhat lower amount of in-person contact between the rural elderly and their children. Smaller population size is also seen as reducing the political clout of rural areas in the competition for program funding at the federal level and increases the cost of available services. This lack of political power reflects a certain degree of invisibility suffered by the rural elderly, who after all represent only one-third to one-quarter of the elderly nationwide. Low population size and heterogeneity may also reduce the ability of rural communities to attract and retain service professionals.

Fourth, although rural areas contain a minority of the elderly in terms of absolute numbers, a greater percentage of the population in rural areas is aged. This is especially true for the North Central region of the country, where 17 percent of the population is aged 65 and over. Thus, North Central rural areas are older than other regions of the country. This would suggest that strains on rural systems related to the needs of the elderly may be particularly burdensome in this region and the South, which has the largest absolute number of rural elderly of any region. The Northeast and West regions, on the other hand, have less than one million rural elderly each. It is clear the age structure of rural areas has been significantly shaped by the out-migration of young adults over the years. During the decade of the 1970's, rural areas in general experienced population growth through in-migration—largely by the young but partially by the old. This occurrence is so recent that its impacts on the rural elderly have only begun to be investigated.

This discussion has highlighted some of the more prominent rural/urban elderly differences and looked at their causes and consequences. It has also revealed that the rural elderly may exhibit many similarities to the elderly living in other environments. Thus, while significant rural/urban elderly differences in a number of areas cannot be ruled out, neither can the alternative hypothesis of no significant rural/urban differences.

A search for a definitive answer to the question of rural/urban elderly differences brings with it a tendency to oversimplify and thus distort reality. The characteristics of the elderly, rural or urban, are complex indeed and affected by a multitude of inter-related factors. In addition, these factors, as well as rural and urban environments, are dynamic, not static, and undergo changes that further complicate the conduct of research analysis and synthesis. A desire to force a conclusion or generalization in regard to a topic on which too little is known is understandable but regrettable.

Thus, a high tolerance for ambiguity may be a prerequisite for those interested in the study of the rural elderly. The topic least plagued by conflicting or inconsistent findings is that of service availability and planning. It is clear that fewer services are made available to the rural elderly in virtually every area and that accessibility to existing services is problematic. In addition, it is clear that service delivery and planning strategies cannot simply consist of watered-down urban models. Rather, innovative programs must be devised that take into account the needs of the rural elderly, the economic, political, and ecological realities of rural places, and the unique characteristics of rural culture and social organization. The following section outlines the need for much greater attention in the area of rural elderly service planning.

CONFRONTING THE CHALLENGE: POLICY AND PLANNING

As this examination of the status of the rural elderly has unfolded, it has become evident from every topic investigated that little if any effort has been made at the federal level to develop a viable policy to address the unique problems of the rural elderly

(Ambrosius, 1979). Wiles (1981) argues that there have been few state-level initiatives to create responsive policies for the rural elderly as well. It was not until the 1978 amendments to the Older Americans Act that the word "rural" even appeared in this legislation. In addition, it would appear that existing programs discriminate against rural areas and do not take into account the demography of the rural environment, its socio-cultural milieu, or its organizational limitations. The small size and low density of rural populations do not support as complex an organizational structure as can be found in metropolitan areas, thus restricting the diversity and availability of services while at the same time increasing costs. This formal organizational structure, limited by local population size and resources as well as inadequate vertical linkages to extra-local institutions, tends to lack the ability to meet existing (to say nothing of future) needs. To the degree that rural service programs are simply "spun off" from metropolitan ones, they run the risk of appearing foreign to rural populations, whose small-town mores and attitudes of distrust toward large bureaucratic institutions should not be ignored.

These observations have important implications for the formulation and implementation of service programs, policy, and delivery strategies directed toward the rural elderly. However, these implications have generally not been translated into workable ideas or incorporated into the existing framework of services for the elderly. A number of concrete suggestions as to how these problems might be addressed have been made by various authors. Steinhauer (1980) argues that policy makers need to address three issues: administration, logistics, and compliance with federal mandates.

Under administrative issues, Nelson (1980) suggests that standards should be set for minimum professional staff size and that appropriate budget allowances should be made for largely rural Area Agencies on Aging (AAA's). Because there is no coordinated system of services for the elderly, policy makers should encourage joint endeavors at the national level (e.g., cooperation between the Farmers Administration and the Health Services Administration) (Green, 1980) and inter-governmental communication at the local level (Ambrosius, 1979). It has also been suggested that a Rural Affairs Unit be established within the

Administration on Aging to elevate the status of the rural elderly in policy considerations (Lane, 1977). Ambrosius (1981), on the other hand, argues that rather than relying on federal agencies, the key to the efficient and effective administration of programs lies in maximally involving elderly constituents and consumers of services. He believes the rural elderly would be better served if AAA's were structured as nonprofit corporations with boards of directors elected by the elderly.

Logistical problems also need to be addressed if service delivery to the rural elderly is to be improved. Steinhauer (1980) suggests that the most fundamental step in this direction involves the recognition that service delivery in rural areas carries a higher unit cost and therefore requires more funding for transportation. A second thrust would be to utilize established, non–elderly-oriented organizations such as cooperative extension services, public schools, and local churches (Coward, 1979). Finally, it has been suggested that the families and friends of the rural elderly could be better incorporated into the formal service delivery structure. This could involve training (and financial support) for the provision of home health and help services (Hayslip et al., 1980).

Problems of compliance with federal mandates can be adequately addressed only through the legislative or regulatory process. However, small changes could be made that would at least improve the ability of rural service agencies to meet federal requirements. Steinhauer (1980) suggests that the skills of rural retirees with professional experience be used to supplement the small staffs of local governments and agencies. A final suggestion is to seek a change in governmental policy to allow AAA's to engage in the direct provision of services. Many rural provider agencies do not have the capabilities to meet the mandates of the Older Americans Act. Several authors (Lane, 1977; Monk, 1977) have argued that monies spent on coordinating services could be used for direct service delivery by these agencies. Other authors have suggested that the current planning system presents somewhat of a no-win situation for rural areas. Lohmann (1982) notes that over 600 AAA's have a uniform planning mandate that is extremely limited in its conception. He argues that rural AAA's do not and cannot carry out effective social planning and that this condition results from the planning model imposed on AAA's by the federal Administration on Aging and the lack of adequate rural resources (Lohmann, 1982). For example, AAA's are prohibited from providing services directly to the elderly and are charged mainly with coordinating services that may not even exist in rural areas. Thus, although perhaps helpful, the suggestions just reviewed may not address the major underlying causes for inadequacies in programs for the rural elderly.

Clearly, more dollars need to be committed at the federal and state levels to develop and maintain programs that respond to the needs of the rural elderly (Kim, 1981; Wiles, 1981). The 1978 amendments to the Older Americans Act did specify that future expenditures in rural areas at the state level were to be at least 105 percent of fiscal year 1978 levels (Ambrosius, 1979). However, this legislation did not clearly indicate whether these services were to be actually located in rural areas or just made available to them, the term "rural" was not defined in the legislation, and no formula was presented for making additional funds available to states with large rural areas (Ambrosius, 1979). But as Shepherd (1984) observes, increased allocations to rural areas will not do much in the way of meeting needs if they are not sensitive to local problems, attitudes, and social structures. Efforts to solve the problem of the rural elderly that simply call for more money or projects, in and of themselves, will do little.

Clearly, these observations and suggestions represent only a small beginning, and a much more comprehensive approach to the organization and provision of services that meets the needs of the rural elderly must be found. As expert observers of the rural scene, gerontologists (be they working directly with the elderly or in academia or government) are in a unique position to contribute to the building of such an approach. It can be said that one measure of the success and usefulness of a field of study is the degree to which it identifies, defines, and provides alternative solutions to social conditions that affect the quality of life of members of a society. Surely, the lack of comprehensive policies and adequate services for the rural elderly is such a condition.

CONCLUDING REMARKS

It has always been traditional (and safe) to end any examination of a topic such as the rural elderly with a lament over the inadequacies of the existing knowledge and a vigorous call for more comprehensive, thorough, and relevant research and analyses. Such a conclusion has never been more appropriate than it is here. Every chapter of this book has demonstrated that fundamental questions concerning the lives of the rural elderly and the problems they face remain unanswered and often unasked. Clearly, more data must be collected on the objective and subjective needs of the rural elderly, the socio-cultural and organizational features of their residential environments, and the ways in which policies and program strategies can be changed to better meet these needs. But before investigators rush off to develop their questionnaires and marshal their research teams, it would seem prudent to take a long, hard look at what such efforts have produced up to now.

The objective of this book was to bring together the very fragmented and often difficult-to-locate literature on the rural elderly to assess what, on the basis of our limited experience, is and is not known about the rural elderly. It is evident from this review that the field has proceeded in such a manner as to make the comparison and integration of research findings, and therefore the building of generalizations, difficult at best. The author contends that gerontologists need to stop and address some very fundamental questions before proceeding with too much more research.

The most basic need is for investigators to develop a typology of rural/urban environments that identifies the factors that impinge directly and indirectly on various aspects of the lives of the elderly. This would require researchers to conceptualize what they mean by "rural" and how they operationalize it. As it stands, the term "rural" is used so sloppily that it is almost impossible to determine what it means. Oftentimes authors do not even inform readers of how they distinguish between "rural" and "urban" for the purpose of their research. Perhaps this practice stems from one of the many myths of the rural elderly—the myth of homogeneity. Nonetheless, the consequence is that elderly populations in many locales get lumped together and called rural. It is hardly to the credit of rural gerontologists or rural sociologists that the term "rural" is so ill defined. One can hardly expect students of aging or policy makers to be impressed with such impreciseness. This is not to say that there is no value in doing studies of older adults whose common characteristic is that they do not live in cities of 50,000 or more. But beyond providing descriptive data, the utility of such studies may be quite limited.

If the term "rural" were used more precisely and with greater attention to its meaning, the state of knowledge of the rural elderly might be better than it is today. By using the term "rural" to refer to such a large universe, the variability that exists between and within rural areas has been obfuscated. The findings of studies that have followed the standard rural/urban dichotomy may accordingly be suspect, and their implications for the question of rural/urban differences should be questioned. Just because an elderly person lives on the outskirts of a central city does not mean that he or she will have similar needs and service use patterns as an elderly counterpart living only several miles away but in the central city. He or she may resemble the elderly living in smaller urban areas more closely.

This review has found that there is variation for the elderly both within and between metropolitan and nonmetropolitan areas and that this variation is both complex and not easily characterized. As a result, not only is the usefulness of this research restricted, but researchers concerned with policy issues and decisions may have inadvertently done the rural elderly a disservice by oversimplifying their complexity and variation. In fact, legislation or service delivery strategies that explicitly incorporate rurality as a unique feature that must be addressed through special initiatives should take this complexity and variation into account. Nonmetropolitan urban versus nonmetropolitan small village and open country and their elderly populations are different and cannot be treated the same, regardless of how convenient doing so may be for setting policy guidelines, funding formulas, or legislative agendas. It would indeed be unfortunate if rural gerontologists unintentionally contributed to this practice by failing to identify and examine how distinctive features of various rural environments interact with other factors to shape the circumstances of the rural elderly.

REFERENCES

Ambrosius, G. 1979, *In Search of a National Policy on the Rural Older Person: An Analysis of the 1978 Amendments to the Older Americans Act*, Council on Aging, University of Kentucky, Lexington, Kentucky.

————. 1981, "To Dream the Impossible Dream: Delivering Coordinated Services to the Rural Elderly," in *Toward Mental Health of the Rural Elderly*, Pikim and C. Wilson (eds.), University Press of America, Washington, D.C.

Coward, R. 1979, "Planning Community Services for the Rural Elderly: Implications from Research," *The Gerontologist*, 19, 275–282.

Green, B. 1980, *New Chances to Expand Rural Health Care: Rural Development Perspectives*, U.S. Department of Agriculture, Washington, D.C.

Hayslip, B., M.L. Ritter, R.M. Oltman, and G. McDonnel. 1980, "Home Care Services and the Rural Elderly," *The Gerontologist*, 20, 192–199.

Kim, P.K. 1981, "The Low Income Rural Elderly: Under-Served Victims of Public Inequity," in *Toward Mental Health of the Rural Elderly*, P. Kim and C. Wilson (eds.), University Press of America, Washington, D.C.

Lane, N.E. 1977, *Speaking Up for the Rural Elderly*, Rural America, Rural America, Washington, D.C.

Lohmann, R. 1982, "Comprehensive What? Coordination of Whom? Rural AAA's and the Planning Mandate," *Journal of Applied Gerontology*, 1, 126–140.

Monk, A. 1977, "Education and the Rural Aged," *Educational Gerontology: An International Quarterly*, 2, 147–156.

Nelson, G. 1980, "Social Services to the Urban and Rural Aged: The Experiences of Area Agencies on Aging," *The Gerontologist*, 20, 200–207.

Shepherd, P. 1984, "Impact of Attitude and Value Structures on the Program Usage of the Rural Elderly," paper presented at the annual meeting of the Gerontological Society of America, San Antonio, Texas, November.

Steinhauer, M.B. 1980, "Obstacles to the Mobilization and Provision of Services to the Rural Elderly," *Educational Gerontology: An International Quarterly*, 5, 399–407.

Wiles, M. 1981, "Providing Human Services to the Rural Elderly: A State Level Perspective," in *Toward Mental Health of the Rural Elderly*, P. Kim and C. Wilson (eds.), University Press of America, Washington, D.C.

INDEX

Aday, R.H., 31
Administration on Aging (AoA), 172–173; and transportation, 115
Age Discrimination Employment Act, 54
Agricultural ladder theory, 252
Ambrosius, G., 172
Area Agencies on Aging (AAA), 144–45, 155, 171–73
Atchley, R.C., 106, 110
Attitudes: leisure services, 60; service provision, 148
Auerbach, A.J., 59, 75

Biegel, D.E., 135
Blacks: income level, 40; number in rural areas, 22; poverty, 42–43
Brody, S., 79
Bultena, G., 92, 125–27, 132
Burkhardt, J.E., 71
Butler, R., 88
Bylund, R.A., 40, 105, 107–8

Carp, F.M., 106
Children. *See* Informal support networks
Church, 172; as leisure activity, 58
Coffin, J., 53
Community structure, and service provision, 148
Comstock, G.W., 90
Cooperative extension service, 172
Cottrell, F., 154
Coward, R.T., 1, 43, 135, 151, 156, 158–59, 161
Crowding, and mental health, 89
Cutler, N., 91
Cutler, S.J., 114

Daatland, S.O., 154
Dahlstein, J., 71
Dean, A., 129
Deimling, G., 125
D'Elia, G., 69, 76
Demography: 15–38; age composition of rural areas, 27; and

informal network support, 132;
migration of elderly, 29–32;
migration patterns in rural
areas, 18, 24, 27–32; number of
elderly in rural areas, 16–19,
27, 31–32; regional variations,
19–22; research needs, 32–33;
rural areas, 169; rural-urban
comparisons, 16–27; sex ratios,
24–25; size of rural population,
2, 15, 16–19; state variations,
19
Diet, 73–74
Divorce, 25–26
Dohrenwend, B.P., 89
Donnenwerth, G., 92
Downing, J., 152

Economic status. *See* Income
Ecosometrics, Inc., 105, 107, 111
Edwards, J., 92
Ellenbogen, B.L., 71
Employment, 51–54; Federal pro-
grams, 52; job deprivation, 56;
research needs, 61–62; satisfac-
tion, 53–54
Escher, M.C., 69
Estes, C., 143

Farmers: career pattern, 52; de-
mography, 18, 53; health, 71–
72; income, 40–41; marital sta-
tus, 24–26; poverty, 44; retire-
ment, 52–56
Farmers Home Administration
(FmHA), 110, 115, 171
Federal legislation, 172
Federal policy, 147, 173
Fengler, A.P., 94
Fertility, 15
Filial responsibility, 130
Flax, J.W., 95
Food assistance programs, 77

Food stamps, 44
Formal services, 143–62; accessibility, 149; and attitudes, 151–
52; availability, 144–46; awareness, 152–53; cost, 159; delivery, 155–57; Federal
expenditures, 147, 173; Federal
programs, 143; focal points,
146; professionals, 147–48; research needs, 157–59; rural
disadvantage, 146–49, 156–57;
utilization, 112, 149–51, 153–54
Fowler, J., 152
Friends. *See* Informal support
networks

Golant, S., 30
Gombeski, W.R., 113–14
Goodfellow, M., 131, 151–54
Government policy and pro-
grams. *See* Formal services
Gowdy, W., 56
Gunter, P.L., 113
Guthrie, H.A., 74, 77

Hargrove, D.S., 95
Harris, A., 57
Harris, M., 52
Health care costs, 76–77
Health care services: accessibil-
ity, 75–78; availability, 75–76;
awareness, 75, 78; Federal, 76,
147; professionals, 76; quality,
76; research needs, 79–80;
transportation problems, 77;
utilization, 78–79
Health insurance, 78
Health maintenance programs,
79
Health problems, 59–73
Health Services Administration,
171
Health status, 67–82; and in-

come, 71; intervening factors, 73; measures, 68–69; research needs, 79–80; research problems, 71–72; rural-urban comparisons, 70–73; self-assessment, 67–69, 74–75
Hirayama, H., 79
Hoar, J., 58
Hospitals. *See* Health care services
House, I., 129
Housing, 103–18; alternatives, 105; characteristics, 105–6; Facility and Condition Index, 107–8; Federal expenditures, 147; importance, 103–4; overcrowding, 106; ownership, 104–5; quality, 106–8; research needs, 115–16
Housing and Urban Development (HUD), 110
Housing programs and services, 108–11
Housing satisfaction, 109
Hughston, G., 58
Human Services. *See* Formal services
Hynson, L., 92–93

Illness, chronic, 59–73
Income, 39–49; adequacy for elderly, 39–40; cost of living, 43, 44; and health care services usage, 77; indicator of well being, 43–45; in-kind, 40; and life satisfaction, 39; programs, 40; research needs, 47–48; satisfaction, 45–47; sources, 41, 44
Informal support networks, 123–37; and health, 129; and life satisfaction, 129; and marital status, 124–25; and migration of youth, 124; neighbors, 123–

24, 130–32; research needs, 132–35; rural-urban comparisons, 124; and service utilization, 154; siblings, 128; stereotypes, 124, 129–30; support for elderly, 128–30; urbanization, 130

Karcher, E.J., 155
Kart, C., 109
Kerckhoff, R.K., 156
Kim, P.K., 41, 76, 147
Kivett, V.R., 45, 53, 55, 57, 60, 69, 71, 75, 113–14, 126–27, 131, 133–34, 153
Krout, J.A., 45, 59, 72, 75, 78, 92, 105, 111, 118, 125, 127, 146, 149, 150–55, 157

Labor force participation. *See* Employment
Larson, D.K., 53, 60, 108, 114
Lassey, M.L., 33
Lassey, W.R., 73, 80
Learner, R.M., 73–74
Lee, G.R., 33, l93, 120, 137
Leisure, 56–61; activities, 56–59, 61; health impact, 59; research needs, 61–62; services, 59–61
Life satisfaction: and mental health, 91; research needs, 95–96; and residence, 91–94; of rural elderly, 8–9; and social interaction, 92, 131
Link, B., 89
Lipman, A., 44
Living arrangements, 26
Lohmann, R., 172
Loneliness, 129, 131
Lopata, H., 152

McCoy, J., 71
McGhee, J.L., 113

McKain, W., 131–32
Marital status: and children, 124–25; rural-urban comparison, 24–26
Marx, K., 46
Mass society, 4
May, A., 150
Means, G., 155
Medicaid, 44, 68, 76, 78, 153
Medical care. *See* Health care services
Medicare, 40, 68, 76, 78, 147
Men: income, 40; leisure activities, 57–58; marital status, 24–26; retirement, 55; rural-urban differences, 24–25; widowerhood, 123
Mental health, 87–98; and age, 87–88, 91; definition of, 87–88; measurement of, 87–88, 91; of rural populations, 88–90
Mental health disorders, 88–89; rural-urban comparisons, 90–91; treatment rates, 89
Mental health services: adequacy, 94; Federal support, 95; lack of professionals, 90–91; research needs, 95–97; rural shortages, 90, 94–95; utilization, 94–95
Mental illness. *See* Mental health
Metropolitan-nonmetropolitan differences. *See* Rural-urban comparisons
Migration: consequences for rural areas, 31–32; and informal support networks, 124–25; post–1970, 2; research needs, 32–33; return, 30; rural to urban, 27–32. *See also* Demography
Miles, L.A., 31
Milgram, S., 4

Moen, E., 151
Montgomery, J.E., 108–9
Mueller, D.P., 90

National Center for Health Statistics, 71
National Council on the Aging, 54
National Rural Strategy Conference, 78, 110–12, 115
Needs assessment, 8
Neighbors. *See* Informal support networks
Nelson, G., 69, 71, 145, 171
New York State Senate, 94–95, 106, 112, 115, 155
Nonmetropolitan, 2–3
Nonmetropolitan population turnaround, 27–32
Norton, L., 74
Nowak, C., 133
Nursing homes, 71
Nutrition, 73–74

Older Americans Act (OAA), 115, 143, 146, 171, 173
Oliver, D.B., 77
Orr, R. H., 112
Ossafsky, J., 40
Ott, C., 157

Palmore, E., 71–72, 77
Paringer, L.J., 71, 73
Parkinson, 149
Patton, C.V., 114
Pfeiffer, E., 88
Pihlblad, C.T., 58
Planning. *See* Formal services
Policy, needs for rural elderly, 170–75
Poverty. *See* Income
Powers, E.A., 114, 127–28, 132, 134, 153

Preston, D.B., 69
Public services. *See* Formal
    services

Quality of life, and migration, 30

Recreation. *See* Leisure
Redick, R., 94
Regions: Great Lakes, 29; Great
    Plains, 29; Midwest, 29; North
    Central, 20–21, 29, 34, 169;
    Northeast, 20–21, 129, 169;
    Ozarks, 29; South, 20–21, 34,
    53, 108, 129, 169; West, 20–21,
    129, 169
Retirement, 51–56; historical
    trends, 51–52; research needs,
    61–62; satisfaction, 55–56; vol-
    untary versus forced, 54
Rowels, G.D., 6
Rural, dimensions of concept, 2–
    3
Rural America, 76, 78, 106–7
Rural areas, 3–6; ecology, 169;
    economy, 168
Rural elderly: disadvantaged sta-
    tus, 7–8; variability, 6–7
Rural-urban comparisons: ade-
    quacy of research, 7–8; cost of
    living, 43–44; employment, 51–
    54; health, 67–82; health care
    personnel, 76; housing, 105–9;
    income, 40–44; informal sup-
    port networks, 131–32; leisure
    activities, 58–59; leisure serv-
    ices, 60–61; life satisfaction, 9,
    91–94; living arrangements, 26;
    marital status, 24–26, 124–25;
    mental health, 88–91; nutri-
    tional status, 73–74; physical
    environment, 5–6; racial com-
    position, 22; retirement, 52–53;

services, 144–56; sex composi-
    tion, 24; transportation, 111–18

Sauer, W., 93, 103
Scheidt, R.J., 87
Schooler, K., 71, 92, 132, 149
Schulte, P., 113
Schwab, J., 90
Schwarzweller, H.K., 31
Scott, J.P., 45, 131
Senior centers: awareness of,
    153; as focal points, 146; and
    leisure activities, 59; rural ver-
    sus urban participation, 150;
    and services, 144, 148, 157
Senior clubs, 152–53
Services. *See* Formal services
Shanas, E., 125
Shepherd, P., 173
Sheps, C.G., 76
Shook, W., 92
Social organization, 60
Social Security Act, 41, 51, 143
Social Security Administration,
    44, 55, 71
Socio-demographic characteris-
    tics, 22–27. *See also*
    Demography
Soldo, B., 106, 143
Srole, L., 89
Standard Metropolitan Statistical
    Area (SMSA), 3
States: Alaska, 21; Arizona, 19,
    69, 75; Colorado, 19, 21; Flor-
    ida, 19, 29, 89, 90; Illinois, 59,
    69, 75–76, 113, 152; Indiana,
    114; Iowa, 21, 127, 132; Kan-
    sas, 21, 94; Kentucky, 45, 53,
    57, 59, 69–70, 75, 77, 92, 108,
    113, 126, 131–32; Louisiana, 19,
    21; Maryland, 19, 21, 90; Mas-
    sachusetts, 21; Mississippi, 58;
    Missouri, 21, 58, 130–31; Ne-

braska, 21; Nevada, 19, 21;
New Mexico, 21; New York,
29, 72, 75, 92, 105, 111–13, 125,
127, 144–46, 149–50, 152–53,
156; North Carolina, 45, 53, 55,
57, 69, 73, 75, 113–14, 126–28,
131, 153; Ohio, 92, 154; Oregon, 19, 92; Pennsylvania,
130–31, 151, 154; Rhode Island,
19; Tennessee, 19; Texas, 113–
14, 131; Vermont, 19, 94; Virginia, 58; Washington, 93;
West Virginia, 19; Wisconsin,
125–26
Steinhauer, M.B., 155, 171–72
Streib, G., 54
Supplemental Security Income
(SSI), 44

Taietz, P., 144–45, 150
Taxes, and home ownership, 105
Telephone: and informal support
networks, 127–28; and service
awareness, 152
Thompson, G.B., 41
Tonnies, F., 3–4
Transportation, 103, 111–18; auto
ownership, 111–12; availability,
111; and informal support networks, 112, 114; impact on leisure activities, 58; and life
satisfaction, 104; and nutritional status, 74; problems,
113–14; programs, 115; research needs, 116–17; and social isolation, 112; and use of
services, 77, 149, 155

United States Bureau of Labor
Standards, 44
United States Bureau of the Cen-
sus, 3, 16–27, 40–41, 106–7,
115, 125
United States Department of
Health, Education, and Wel-
fare (HEW), 147
Urbanized area, definition of, 16
Urban Institute, 72
Urban Mass Transportation
(UMTA), 115

Values, 4–5, 77, 124

Wade, S., 130
Ward, R.A., 131
Weeks, J., 54, 91
White House Conference on the
Aging, 88, 94, 104, 111, 115
Widowhood, 20, 24, 114
Wildovsky, A., 80
Wiles, M., 171
Windley, P.G., 149
Wirth, L., 4, 89
Women: income, 40; informal
support networks, 129; leisure
activities, 57–58; marital status,
24–26; retirement, 55; rural-ur-
ban differences, 24–25; trans-
portation problems, 112, 114;
widowhood, 123
Work satisfaction. See
Employment

Youmans, E.G., 40, 45, 57, 69–
70, 75, 77–78, 92, 126–27

ABOUT THE AUTHOR

JOHN A. KROUT is Associate Professor of Sociology and Director of Sponsored Research at the State University of New York at Fredonia. He has contributed articles on a variety of issues regarding the elderly to a number of journals, including *The Gerontologist, Research on Aging, Social Services Review,* and *The International Journal of Aging and Human Development.* He has presented numerous papers on the rural elderly at professional conferences and recently published a reference work on this topic titled *The Rural Elderly: An Annotated Bibliography of Social Science Research.* His research on the rural elderly has been supported by a grant from the Administration on Aging and several awards from the American Association of Retired Persons' Andrus Foundation.